THE PULSE OF CREATION SERIES

THE VOICE OF HERMES

THE

VOICE OF HERMES

Clairvoyantly and Clairaudiently Received

through

ERNEST L. NORMAN

The Third Volume of

THE PULSE OF CREATION

UNARIUS
EDUCATIONAL FOUNDATION
145 S. Magnolia Avenue
El Cajon, California 92020

THIRD EDITION

Printed in Hong Kong

ISBN 0-932642-02-0

Unarius Educational Foundation
El Cajon, California, 92020

FOREWORD

We present to you "The Voice of Hermes" which, as one of the seven books of "The Pulse of Creation" series, represents part of the culminative efforts of many thousands of advanced souls living in the Higher Spiritual Planes of life. We can therefore in this presentation be pardoned for any feelings of pride in accomplishment, for indeed these works do and will represent to so many thousands of persons in the present and future time to come, a *new way of life,* an inward realization of hopes, aspirations, and visions, which, in its fulfillment will free them from the dogmatic systems, material strifes, and various derelictions of the earthly world.

The completion of any one or all of the works of Unarius is a story which reads like some of the fantastic classical epilogues which have been immortalized from the minds of great literates of the past; yet, unlike these classical portrayals, there is nothing fantastic, unreal, or fictional in these works, but rather a miraculous joining and union of great periods of time, wherein the aspiration and ideals of the higher life could be brought into fruition by the inner self.

To create even a simple book is not an easy task, and is complicated a thousand fold when considered that in these books of Unarius, there is an accumulated wisdom, not only from the past ages of time, but sufficient of this Higher Wisdom to prepare man for his journey into the future.

Yes indeed, the story of Unarius is one which would transcend all known boundaries and the limits of presently existing classical literature. Romantic indeed, in some aspects, is the story of Ruth and Ernest, which reads much like the quest of some Galahad in search of the Holy Grail; and, like some knighted Lancelot of the past in quest of some fair Elaine, so it was with Ernest, who for some fifteen years searched for Ruth, knowing not of her exact whereabouts, but often describing her to many people, telling them that she alone could make him and his work whole. And so the day came to pass that, wherein certain earthly cycles had been lived and justified and with an almost uncanny split second timing, these two were joined and the great work began.

Yet it was not all smooth sailing from the start. There were still many things to be worked out; habits, personal traits of character had to be changed. But more important, a better attunement was gradually made with the *Higher Self* of these two individuals. Thus it can be said that Ruth and Ernest represent an inspiring example to those who seek a better *Way;* for they have succeeded in some small or large measure in freeing themselves from the *pits of clay* which are indigenous to most earthly people; and they have succeeded in helping many others also to free themselves.

To describe the actual process of creating these books means the common joining of many minds, and consistent and seemingly never-ending persistence in so many ways. First the context material must be transcribed onto the magnetic tape. This is done through the channelship as it is represented by Ernest. This, too, means joining together, under selected conditions, the culminative efforts of so many thousands of spiritual souls, who, through the mind and vocal cords of the channel, energize the necessary impulses on the magnetic tape.

Then come the long processes of transcribing this material, word for word, onto the type written page; then careful editing and re-editing, consideration always being given that nothing shall be deleted, the delicate fabric of the transcendent power always being kept interwoven with these word forms and pictures.

Here, honorable mention should be made to those who have assisted so nobly in this task. To Ruth, who not only furnishes a positive and guiding power in these earthly dispensations, but who finds in her spiritual transcendency, numerous ways in her daily life, to dispense her new found Light to others. *

To Velma Wasdell, a dedicated soul, who, coming out of the past and her previous associations with the beginnings of Unarius, is now again following the true path, and in her talented efforts as a professional editor, has contributed much to this work.

There are others too, one who wishes to remain anonymous, but whose efforts also in so many ways have earned for her the name "Blessing."

Another, too, whose great talent graces the pages of this book in the form of the various illustrations, is Carlos Leberman, who at one time was internationally known as an artist and who illustrated many other books, such as "The Earth Dweller Returns". It is in Carlos that we have found a true artist, as he too, like many of the others, have come out of the past in numerous contacts and associations with us in the beginnings of Unarius; and is thus able to directly portray a certain inspired measure of the transcendent beauty which is found in these higher spiritual planes. Carlos, too, is again walking the *path,* and finds that, day by day, the material world is receding far into the distant past.

It must not be considered that the works of Unarius represent just another escape mechanism which would find a universal appeal to those in dire straits and circumstances who are seeking an easy way out. It should first be considered that Unarius teaches people a better *Way*, for it must be understood that the material world as it is now presented, either from the present or the past, is only the beginning of any man's evolution, from the primitive reaches and beginnings of his existence which can be called man, wherein he is starting that never-ending cycular pattern of interplay with the *Infinite Creative Substance* of all the seen and invisible cosmos.

And in this concept Unarius is diametrically opposed to any materialistic concept, which tends to equate the world as the sum and total of all things. Neither does Unarius support the religionist, whose approach to the Infinite is, in his religion, purely an escape mechanism, and in his deistic attitudes, is only portraying another readapted form of the many paganisms in which he has engulfed himself in past life times.

Therefore the reader and student must fully realize his own moral responsibility in his position with the *Creative Infinite Mind;* that his present position is the accumulation of the past, and that conversely he must, if not satisfied with this position, obviously change it, as his present position is actually the interwoven matrix of energy wave forms which he has composed from past life experiences.

It is equally obvious that no one but himself can change these things for him. How this is done and the inclusion of all other necessary concepts and various introspective additives, are all presented in these works to the truth seeker who wishes not an escape mechanism but a *"New Way of Life"*, which will be composed of various attributes which will thus express a greater degree of perfection.

Scientifically, philosophically, and in many other comparative forms of retrospection, the student will find in these works, all the necessary constituents and attributes for this, *"New Way"*. He can thus begin to build his *new life* and, with a dedicated patience, which, when extended into the future, and his many thousands of lives, will thus completely reconstitute this person who has so dedicated himself.

As Jesus said, "Seek and ye shall find; knock and the door shall be opened," but let this seeking and knocking and opening be of your own doing, for *no man* doeth unto another that which he cannot do for himself.

We, the channels of Unarius, do dedicate these works to the honest and sincere seeker, knowing that he too, just as we have and are so doing, will find his *new Way of Life,* and as ye do so, so it shall be added unto you.

* It was Ruth, too who, also through inner guidance, found the way for Unarius to print its own books; and it is she who prepares the final script on the complex typewriter-like mechanism known as the Vari-typer. The final duplicating process called offsetting is being done by a large commerical house which specializes in this work. As a note of interest, Ruth learned not only typewriting but also the more complex Vari-typing procedures while she was physically asleep, her true self thus being taught in the spiritual classrooms associated with Unarius and she has in these capacities completely vindicated a cardinal principle contained in the concepts of Unarius. At the present time her typing is a rapid fire staccato manipulation of the keys, and is entirely an independent function from the conscious mind, her only problem being, as she expressed it, to keep her mind off the machine. This then can be considered independent writing as a normal physical function, powered and motivated from the Higher Self.

Look Thee
Unto the Stars
And That They Endureth
Forever
For Surely Then
As These Stars Are
Created Like Unto Thine
Own Suns and Planets
And As Thou Hast Has Found
A Home Among Them
Surely Then of the Many
Stars Which Are Countless
And Without Number
Thou Wilt Find
Thy New Home
And in the Finding
Adding Unto It
More of the Glory
Of Heaven.

CHAPTER 59

A most fond and hearty greeting to you, brother and sister. I formerly lived on the earth at about the turn of the sixteenth century, in the country of Holland, and was known as Anton Leeuwenhoek. With the help of some of my worthy colleagues, I shall attempt to resume our transmission into further studies of philosophical arts and sciences and of the differences in the philosophical interpretations in the various ages as they have existed on your earth. However, before we get directly into this subject, may I say that it is a particularly gala occasion, not only for myself but for another of my very fond and worthy brothers by the name of Galileo. It is we two who have associated ourselves with you in a personal way as spiritual god-fathers through your earth plane life in this reincarnation: and we have been quite successful in stimulating your interests in such subjects as have been relative to your own earth plane expressions.

However, I could go even farther than that. Some time ago, before your reincarnation on the earth in your present life, you were with us here in Aureleus, at which time we laid down somewhat the pattern or foundation for your expression of the philosophical arts and sciences and in the explanations of the so-called esoterical interpretations as they are now being given to you from the seven centers of Shamballa. Being so closely associated with you in your earth life, may I also say that there have been several spiritually minded people who have seen us in your proximity at different times, as long white-bearded men with large books. So that you would know us better, we appeared to these people thusly; however, as you see me now, the question of whether I have a beard is something you could not solve, for appearance here in these spiritual dimensions, with clairvoyance as you now possess, is sometimes rather difficult, since clairvoyance begins on a new threshold of conception.

I see you are standing here in the great central section of the park-like area which surrounds the central temple of Aureleus; and immediately in front of you is a beautiful building called the Temple of Apollo. Since it related to the Golden Age of Grecian philosophy, we can go directly into this subject for a two fold purpose; for in explaining to the student the philosophies and ages in which they existed, the student may better be able to judge for himself the values of such philosophies as they relate to his own particular dimension. There are actually no strong lines of demarcation, or, I might say, expression in philosophical fields, even in the most elemental of the philosophies of the earth; and while each individual has his own philosophy, no two of these compositions are the same; yet basically there are elements of spiritual values interwoven into each person's philosophy, which relate him into the more immediate spiritual dimensions and realms. In other words, even the savage or bushman living in the primitive reaches of the earth is so concerned in his own mind with spirits or such forces of nature that he trembles in superstitious awe at any supernatural phenomenon which he may witness during his lifetime; and even the rabbi or the priest of the temple expresses a sense of philosophy in his own particular dimension.

We can begin our discussion here by looking more closely at the Temple of Apollo, as it existed on the earth about 550 years before Christ. It is of pure Doric architecture, which is quite similar to many of the buildings and structures or churches and cathedrals on the earth, either in the present or past histories. I have always been amazed at the fact that usually the builders, whether emperors, kings or spiritual leaders, have first constructed these cathedrals or temples in the spiritual domains before they reincarnated into the earth, where they would rebuild the temple with which they were familiar from their spiritual domain; and in the remaining years of their life on the earth, they would fill the temple or building with the work that contributed to the posterity of mankind. Such an example was Solomon himself, for he was quite familiar with, and very useful in helping to construct the great central temple here in Aureleus; consequently, later in his reincarnation, he constructed a smaller but rather similar model of this temple in the Holy Land of Judea.

The Golden Age of Grecian philosophy begins about 1000 years before Christ, with the advent of the blind poet and bard, Homer. He was a wandering minstrel in the early period of his life, traveling around Asia Minor throughout the Grecian Peninsula; and he compounded such immortal verses as the Iliad and the Odyssey, in which he portrayed the life of a Grecian king, named Ulysses, in the quest of Troy. About 200 years after the passing of Homer, we find that the people of Greece were compounded of three definite races, the Aeolians, the Dorians, and the Ionians, who were so interwoven in their social structures that they later became known as the Hellenic people or the Hellenes, as they liked to be called. In the earlier stages of their development, their temples were very often expressed in the Doric type of architecture.

This, you will note rather closely, is somewhat reminiscent of the Egyptian architecture with the fluted columns and the lintels, which the columns support over the great massive doorways which are sometimes attached, or, at other times, with a compound of squares and arches. The Doric column is a more primitive or an earlier expression of art. The fluted columns end in a simple scroll-like design. A little later version of the column was the Ionic, somewhat higher, more slender and tapering, with double flutes. A still later version came from the culture of Corinth, and was therefore called the Corinthian type of architecture, which embodied a very intricate design at the top of the column, embellished with interwoven leaves of the anthemion and various other intricate scroll-like designs. Altogether, these temples are very beautiful in their utmost simplicity and charm. Here in Aureleus they serve a dual purpose for the student and the teacher, where both may thus correlate their pursuance of these philosophical sciences in a proper and suitable environment which best stimulates the more fertile and imaginative processes of the mentality; for at the time of the building of the Temple of Apollo in Corinth, in about 560 B.C., the Golden Age of Grecian philosophy was perhaps at its height.

It was somewhere in the vicinity of this time that the great masters of the Grecian philosophies existed and taught in their different academies. The backbone of the structures of Grecian philosophy extends from the exponents whom you know as Aristotle, Socrates, Plato, and Pythagoras. Of course, there are dozens of others of lesser mental stature and not so well known in the bibliography of history. However, they too played an important part in various classical interpretations of Greek art, philosophies, and sciences.

Now we shall walk down the main thoroughfare and enter this huge Corinthian temple of Pericles which actually existed in Athens. Pericles, as you know, was a great Athenian statesman as well as a philosopher of no mean sort; and it was under his righteous rule and government that the Grecian Hellenic Age flourished into its greatest maturity. Compounded in this temple we shall find the works, not only of the greater of the Grecian philosophers, but also of some of the lesser. At this time the age of philosophy was one which compounded many other attributes of philosophy, materialistic, mental, and spiritual into the daily lives of the Grecian subjects. Greece was a very highly developed and cultured country. It flourished at the height of its culture and glory while Rome was yet but a collection of huts, clustered together on the seven hills of the Tiber River. Rome, as you know, was started somewhere about 600 B.C., by the twins, Romulus and Remus, who were fostered by a she-wolf, according to the histories of the earth; however, I personally can take this or leave it.

We know Rome rose rapidly into the foreground as one of the greatest nations and empires of the world and, as such, completely conquered and overran the countries in the Mediterranean area, including Greece; however, here is a case of the story of the two snakes, each one trying to swallow the other by the tail. Whether Greece conquered Rome or whether Rome conquered Greece, to distinguish between the two was difficult; for at the time of the Roman invasion, Rome was greatly infused by the civilization of Greece. Studying the history of Greece in itself reveals

470

many great and wonderful facts. The cities of Alexandria, of Corinth, of Athens, of Olympus, and many others in the shadow of the Twin Peaks of Copernicus are related to the period of Pericles in the classics of Greek history. The Pantheon of the Greek gods stemmed from Jupiter, or Zeus—also known as Theseus—in the great temple of Olympia, which supposedly existed on the top of this great Mount of Copernicus. The Greek gods and goddesses were expressed as Athena, Poseidon, Hermes, Apollo, Baccus, and many others, too numerous to mention at this time. Your earth histories would serve you here if you wish to know more about them; however, they are familiar even to the student in high school.

Now it so happens in your modern world that the academies and universities teach these Grecian philosophies, sometimes in their pure Grecian language, and they hold them in some kind of secular or votive reverence. These philosophies, as was explained by Copernicus, were very valuable and relevant in their time and place; yet with the passing of time, sometimes certain elements of these philosophies have been proved to be untrue, or should be modified. An example of this exists in the story of Aristotle and the theory of the pendulum, which was later disproved by Galileo, who watched the pendulum swinging in the drafty loft of a huge cathedral of his native Italy. There he counted the movements of these long and short pendulums, which swung as chandeliers in this great church, noting and timing the movements of the pendulums with the pulse of his wrist; thus he was able to upset completely the entire theory of pendular motion, as expounded by Aristotle. Likewise some of the higher orders of mathematics and calculus have in your day and age been modified and disproved by Einstein, another exponent of science.

What I mean by all this is, of course, that we simply must not take philosophy at its face value. Such elements as are compounded in these philosophies should be carefully weighed and extracted and used only in their proper position and in their proper time and place; such factors as relate their usage to your own particular environment, your understanding of life, and in the principles and in the equations which enter into such formula or the various facets which are transversing about you in the historical pageantry of time.

Now passing down through the age of the Grecian philosophies and into the time of the advent of Christ, we find that there had been some new developments on the religious or esoterical fields throughout the Mediterranean countries, particularly in Greece. One of these cults was called Mithraism, which was a direct outgrowth of the Zoroastrian concept, which had been expounded in Persia with the advent of the prophet Zoroaster. Mithraism was very attractive, inasmuch as it offered a large amount of pomp and circumstance, various observances and ceremonies, all of which were quite attractive to the people of that time. Other orders included the rabbinical orders of the Essenes, which stemmed from the more ancient Hebraic concepts from the Holy Land. We also find at that time a large group which was growing out of some of the lighter orders of Christian concepts, known as the Gnostics, who were spiritually minded people who believed that the true wisdom and knowledge and interpretations of life stemmed directly from the inward consciousness of man.

Beginning somewhere about twenty or thirty years after the time of Jesus, we find Paul in Greece very busily at work. It had been some time since his conversion on the road to Damascus; and he had already lived some time in Corinth and written some of his very famous letters to the people of that city. These letters and teachings exist in the modern translations of the New Testament. Paul, as you know, was formerly anti-Christ and persecuted the Christians to the utmost of his ability until his conversion. It was Paul who started the first Christian church; and as Paul was also a very clever businessman in his own way, he realized that religion, just as anything else, should be attractive and should present certain aspects to the convert; consequently, he contrived to weave the concepts of Mithraism into his own Christian church. Thus he proselyted the Mithraic and the Grecian pantheon of numerous converts and attracted them into his own church. I might say that some of the adopted concepts included observances of the Spring Equinox or the Festival of the Taurobolium, which was the slaying of the black bull by Ahuramazda, and the three day retirement and the resurrection also, just as was found in many other religious observances and cults.

The winter solstice of December the twenty-first to the twenty-fifth of that month was a time of religious observances, climaxed by indulgences on the twenty-fifth. This later became the birthday of the Christ; and the story of the immaculate conception, just as it existed with the concept of Zoroaster, was here interwoven into the Christian philosophies of the origin of the Christian religion. With the death of Paul, the Christian Church split into two factions —the one faction remaining in Greece as a Greek orthodox, which later developed into the Byzantine Empire. The other which was under direct supervision of Peter, with headquarters in Rome, became later known as the Holy Catholic Church or, as it was called in those days, the Christian Church.

So for over 200 years, this church, under the supervision of those who followed after Peter, suffered severe persecutions from the Romans. The Christians were fed to the lions and were burned at the stake and suffered other innumerable martyrdoms, until the advent of the Emperor Constantine, who became converted to Christianity and issued the Milan Edict, which not only made Christianity lawful and legal, but placed it under the direct protectorate of the Roman Emperor himself. Funds were donated to build churches and otherwise to promote the growth of the Christian Church.

Thus entered a phase of history known as the Holy Roman Empire; and thus under the numerous Roman Emperors who came up during the hundreds of years following Constantine, it was a question whether the later version of the Roman Catholic Church, which began to be headed by an individual known as the Pope, or whether the Emperor of Rome himself ruled the Roman Church. As it was known, the Holy Roman Empire came into such strength and dominion that it overran and overruled the entire western continent of Europe; and by the time of Otto the First, in the year 800 A.D., it was completely and thoroughly entrenched in all countries. At about the time of the twelfth and the thirteenth centuries, this Holy Roman Empire had gathered such strength that it ruled the destinies of the small and the great. Kings and queens trembled at the Pope's name, and no one dared act unless he knew that it would be thoroughly approved by the visionaries in Rome. The Pope literally held the keys to heaven and hell for every individual.

Confession was mandatory at regular intervals. It was so, too, that the various ecclesiastical orders were also in great preponderance and abundance.

Fat monks waddled up and down the highways and byways and streets of every country in Europe; nuns, too, from the various cloistered convents were numerous and made their appearance in countless and diverse places. It was so that the individual who worked for his living, a tradesman or yeoman, was subjected to various tithes or taxations, which reduced him to even a lower existence or level; so that gradually the wealth of these countries of Europe was being absorbed into coffers of the church.

Now it is so conceived that such tyranny and such oppression must be relieved. The ultimate destiny of mankind is not to be long overridden or overburdened by such tyrannical oppression. The very soul of man himself will, under such pressure, scream to the high heavens for relief. Thus it was that the great Shamballa, headed by the planet Eros, swung into action; and for the next five or six hundred years, the planet earth was at different times literally showered with the illustrious names of many thousands of individuals, who each contributed in a large and small part to the liberation of mankind from the tyranny of the Holy Roman Empire. This was the period known as the Reformation; and is also known as the Inquisition, with the writhing and squirming of the minds of men for liberation as came the writhings and squirmings of the Papal orders which took all manner of means to suppress any outbreaks. Consequently, in the coming several hundred years and in my time, we saw literally hundreds of thousands of people burned at the stake; others were thrown into dungeons or broken upon the rack or the wheel, or excommunicated and sent into exile. Sometimes their businesses and fortunes were confiscated and their families and homes broken and sent into disgrace. These periods of inquisition were written as some of the blackest blotches upon the pages of history. I might also say that some of the brightest pages of history are lying side by side with the black ones, written with the words and signed by the names of these illustrious personages who incarnated into your earth at that time.

I could name a few of these very luminous minds, starting with Francis Bacon, in the field of literary expressions; and around and about his time came others, such as Wycliffe, and a Scotsman by the name of John Knox. Then everyone knows of Martin Luther and his holy insurrection against the Holy Roman Empire. There were others, too, who manifested a great deal of influence; John and Charles Wesley, who started the religious order known as Methodism; William Penn, who migrated with his converts and followers to America, in seeking his religious freedom. In fact, the Thirteen Colonies were originally founded by such religious refugees as the Puritans, who sought religious sanctuary in the far-off land across the sea, away from the oppressive dominion of the Catholic Church or the Church of England.

There were other expressions, too, which illuminated and typified the struggle for the rise of mental and spiritual stature and nature of man at that time. In the poetry of that time, we find such great masters as Goethe, Chaucer, Browning, Tennyson, Gray, Keats, all of these men and many more, and shall I say women also, referring to Elizabeth, who lent a small voice; and although they did not outwardly castigate or exorcise the Roman Empire and its Holy Church, yet their works were no less conducive to the liberation of the consciousness of man into a higher trend of spiritual concept. For myself, I fortunately contributed something to the world of science, and as a former draper, I was interested in lenses; and in the magnifications of the first crude lenses which I ground, and so contrived the first model of my first microscope, which was simply a pinhole drilled through a piece of brass whereon a tiny droplet of water was suspended. Peering through this tiny hole at some object immediately below, the drop of water gave some sort of distorted magnification. Later on I developed a way to grind lenses and mount them in the turret heads of an instrument, which was the forerunner of your modern microscope; and I managed to achieve magnifications which enabled me to inspect some of the microscopic domain, called bacteria, protozoans, cells, and various other types of heretofore unseen and unknown structures in the world about us.

Far to the south of me in the sunny land of Italy was my dear friend Galileo, who brought into expression the first usable refractory telescope and thus he explored the heavens to verify further the findings of Copernicus, who placed the earth in its proper orbit around the sun and thereby explored the immediate reaches of the great celestial and terrestrial universes about us. Incidentally, I might say that Galileo found in his small telescope that there were something like 300 or 400 million suns or stars, which the modern astronomers have been able to catalogue. It is at this present time estimated that these various stars or suns in the terrestrial universe number over a hundred trillion. However, do not pay too much attention to these astronomical figures; a trillion or a billion means little to the average person. In some future day when you have elevated into a concept of truth and light, you will be able to see a much larger portion, not only of the terrestrial, but also of the celestial universe.

Now getting back to our original discussion in

this great age of reformation and liberation. The field of music was also very fortunately blessed with a flood of personages from the planes of Shamballa. What other age has produced such names as Brahms, Beethoven, Bach, Mozart, Mendelssohn, Chopin, Liszt? The age of opera, as it came into being then, has never before been equaled in the history of the earth. The musical composers and exponents of these operatic arts, known by the names of Puccini, Poncelli, are but a few illustrious names, if you will pardon me for mentioning them again, who have been given in previous transmissions; however, all of this must be brought out and favorably placed at this time; so please bear with me. In the more pure philosophical vein, we find great and luminous minds typified by Leibnitz, John Locke, Emanuel Swedenborg, Immanuel Kant, Mesmer, Hartley, Descarte, Condorcet, Carlyle, Emerson, Hume, etc. Incidentally, your own American philosopher is here with me this evening, standing by in your dimension and helping to interpret my little speech.

Emerson was very vitally connected with your father in his earth life reincarnation, and they are very closely connected in a friendly way in Aureleus. May I add, too, that your father has met Emanuel Swedenborg and is very happy at the occasion to be constantly in his company; and do not feel a loss, for I caught your thought immediately. I may say that you also were quite close to Swedenborg in a previous reincarnation on the earth plane; and you are largely expressing, just as he did, some of the unfinished philosophies and works in the spiritual domain, which he was unable to complete fully or to explain at his time. It is your previous training and work on the earth at this time which is enabling Swedenborg to gain a great deal of happiness, because your being on the earth now was very carefully planned, and is vitally pertinent to the time and place of evolution in the history of the world, as it is transpiring at the present time.

Do not be alarmed if your writing and work and collaborations at the present time do not meet with the outstanding success which you anticipate; but rest assured that they will be a very definite part of the basic spiritual structures of the world to come. Thus, you see your work is not only of yourself; rather it is a great plan and a collaboration of these great luminous minds which lived in the period of Reformation in the fifteenth, sixteenth, and seventeenth centuries. It matters little that you could be called a reincarnation of Swedenborg; but it matters much that the truths and philosophies in which you and Swedenborg are so vitally interested and concerned in spreading in the world are necessarily expounded at this particular time and place. That is of utmost importance; personalities fall by the wayside. It was no happenstance that you were born into the family and into the period of time nor that your father almost immediately took up the study of the philosophy of Swedenborg through the many years of your childhood. You were spiritually in contact with your very worthy colleagues here in Aureleus, as you left us to migrate to the earth. For your own part as a personality, I would say that you too, although I will not tell you of such identity, were and are one of the minds of whom I have spoken in the previous age; that you have lived in other incarnations in history to bring into the expression of mankind at that particular moment, some segment or fragment of truth that would best serve man in his own place.

Now in our discussion of the philosophers in our period of Reformation, for obvious reasons I could mention only a small number; however, some of the more prominent names I have given. Spinoza was also one who contributed a great deal of wealth to the philosophical world. If you study the various philosophies of these different minds and individuals, you will find that there are rather wide differences. For instance, John Locke is credited with being the Father of Empiricism, in which he expressed the concept of man as coming into the world with a blank mind, upon which the experiences and the relationships of his experiences upon the earth related him into his intelligent and functional pattern of Life. This in itself has contributed something to your present science of psychiatry and psychology. However, it does not go into the more purely spiritual dimensions as expressed by Swedenborg, who was factual enough to say that the soul did not exist in the body; instead man was so integrated with the supreme spiritual consciousness of God Himself that many experiences or facets of his individual life were contrived by Divine expression. We could say with Leibnitz, who postulated his monadic theory, that here again man was God Himself expressing himself in the inward consciousness in a different way.

If we examine the philosophies of Jesus, here too we find the inward consciousness, the continuity of intelligence, as expressed from the inward nature of man himself into the higher celestial dimensions of the universal spiritual world about him. Now, other obvious facts remain with the study and pursuance of the philosophical ideologies of these different personages. Even though the philosophy of Jesus himself was not sufficient to satisfy the needs of the whole world, yet it has remained the one philosophy which has exerted the greatest influence over the greatest numbers and masses of people and has endured for a longer time than has any other philosophy.

However, for each Christian, there may be a thousand or more people of different nationalities or races who never heard of Christ and who derive their spiritual inspirations from Buddha or Krishna or Mohammed or some other spiritual personage. Perhaps Zoroaster or some derivative of the Zoroastrian concept influences the motivations and purposes of many individuals or races of people. Here again we must draw a parallel and in studying the philosophies and spiritual ideologies, compounded into these various factional expressions, we are struck by this strange parallel: all cases with the highest expression of the spiritual virtues bear a striking similarity, and therefore they may be said to spring from the one eminent source. So who is to challenge the question of whether it is Buddha, Mohammed, or Christ.

All in all, we must say that man, in his destiny, relies more purely on his inward consciousness and his inward attunement in relating himself to the higher dimensions and realms of life; and in such relationships he comes into the fullest and most conscious expression and concept in his evolution. Consequently, I might say to those who would read these lines, for even in your day, there are many who are clamoring loudly from the steps of their various churches, with or without spires, from the tents of their revivalist meetings, or from other rabbinical structures that you can find your salvation only through the doorway of this temple or that shrine.

Heed not the cry of the exponent, for he himself must find a new doorway before he can enter the Kingdom of Heaven. To the priest or religious expressionist, I may say that individually or personally you will never come to the end of your evolution of time; nor will you see the end of the various derivations of philosophies and esoterical ideologies which relate you to these different spiritual dimensions.

No, friends, the end will not be in sight for thousands, yea, hundreds of thousands of years; so look not for salvation in this your own present life nor in the different evolutions to come. Your own salvation remains entirely upon the concept of the life force which is within you, the force which comes from the great Central Fountainhead, the Life Force of God himself. Do not think that I am saying that you should not heed the works or read the words of wisdom and knowledge as they are contained and compounded the books and philosophies which exist on the earth plane; as Kung Fu would say, "The longest journey begins with the first step." Each one in his soul evolution must begin first to learn to think constructively by beginning constructive and intelligent evaluation of life principles as they exist within his own mentality.

So, friends and dear ones, read the books of the great libraries, the academies, and the universities of the earth plane. Listen to the words of knowledge and wisdom which come from the temples and from the other places; and although they may be words of wisdom and they may be truths which are compounded in your world and in your time, yet they are only as small stones at your feet on the pathway of life. They must be properly understood and evaluated, otherwise they could seriously impede your progress, for it is thus conceived in the Divine Mind that each man must find his own pathway, his own evolution.

So until such further time, I am very grateful to be of assistance in expressing some of the concepts and some of the knowledge which we have found to exist in the spiritual side of life from one of the centers of Shamballa. I give my humble observance and grati-

482

tude to the collaborators in this transmission: Maha Cohan, Gamaliel, Ralph Waldo Emerson, and others for helping me to integrate, to inspire, and to stimulate your mind in the process of reason and wisdom, so that this transmission could be fully contained and recorded. Until such further time, your very loving friend and brother.

— Anton.

CHAPTER 60

I am Galileo and this is a most happy occasion to contact the earth again. I lived in the Italian town of Pisa in Italy around the sixteenth century. In referring to your history books, you will find that I was born in a poor but very noble family, achieved some success as a mathematician, and was credited with the invention of the telescope; however, that is not quite correct. Much work was done by some very eminent earth people before my time in the grinding and polishing of lenses and in the formulation of optical laws and principles of diffusion and diffraction. It was, however, my good fortune to be able further to expound and rediscover some of the mathematical principle of law and motion which were enlarged and enriched by Sir Isaac Newton at a somewhat later date.

I see that we are still standing in the great temple of Pericles here in Aureleus; and while you are becoming accustomed to and gaining some composure in your strange environment I shall relate a little more of my own personal history at the time of my living on the earth planet. Now, as Anton told you, it was a very dangerous age, and one in which one who expounded new truths was in grave danger of losing his life; for anyone who dared to think or act differently from the clergy or the priesthood of the Roman Imperial Church was usually accused of high treason and thrown into a dungeon to await some very dire fate. At the earliest possible moment I became a professor on the faculty at the University of Padua, Italy, and taught subjects which were related to mathematics, physics, and the physical sciences.

It was during these years that I was able to construct a reasonably good working telescope of the refractory design; and although it may have been crude as compared with some of the instruments of your day, yet it enabled me to explore somewhat in the vicinity of this great terrestrial universe and to verify the findings of Copernicus.

Until this time the Holy Roman Empire and the various high officials of the world in which I lived believed in the old Ptolemaic theory that the earth was the center of the universe and that all heavenly bodies swung in orbits around it. With the aid of my telescope I was able to verify the findings of my very worthy colleague, Copernicus. I became very jubilant about these findings; and because I was an enthusiastic person in those days, I talked very loudly about these things until my findings fell upon wrong ears, after which I was finally arrested and thrown into a very dirty filthy dungeon. Now, this place was horrible beyond description; and I witnessed the poor wretches being brought in day after day, some of whom were led away to be burned at the stake or to be further tortured into admission of sins and guilt on the rack and the wheel; whether they were innocent or not made little or no difference; they were always condemned. You can sympathize with me very greatly; I reasoned to myself that a dead Galileo would be of no use to the earth; consequently, I publicly recanted and got down on my knees before the fat bishops and told them that I had made a very terrible mistake. However, that did not change my ideas one whit; and again I went about my work, only to be re-arrested a couple of years later. Nothing but the intercessions of my very best friends and the fact that I had been of noble birth saved me that time. Please be sympathetic with me, my friends; could I be accused of some sort of prevarication or guile since I could smell the stench of burning flesh and hear the screams of the poor wretches, as they were burned in the courtyard above the grated cell in my dungeon?

Now you have looked about you, with Anton. Here in this great Temple of Pericles, you have seen that it was devoted more or less to its historical value as the epitome of Grecian culture shortly before the advent of Jesus, when the good Emperor Pericles had erected it for posterity in the philosophical arts and sciences; and it is quite logical that such usages should be continued here in Aureleus. We shall look about us a little and examine some of the classrooms, to see who it is that is teaching the various kinds of philosophies which are being expounded in this beautiful Grecian temple. Some of the more well known Greek philosophers were previously mentioned; however, there are also many others you might care to examine in your history books, containing common factual knowledge as taught in most of the academies and universities, others who also contributed considerable wealth of knowledge and wisdom into the philosophical arts and sciences of that age. I might mention a few more, such as Demosthenes, Plutarch, Ptolemy, Democritus, Xenophanes, Epicurus, Euripides, and a host of others.

However, for the sake of convenience for the moment, let us just step through this beautiful ornate arched doorway into this classroom, which is at the present time being conducted by Democritus. He is a Grecian philosopher who had a very highly advanced theory of atomic structures, amazingly similar to the

486

one expounded by your present day physical scientists. He explained the core or nucleus of matter as consisting of tiny atomic particles, and gave much to the theory and content of their construction and to their function.

As you look into this classroom, you will see it is quite a large beautiful dome-shaped building, the Radiant Energies of which seem to be pulsating in the ceiling and through the prism like structures which always seem to be indigenous with these classrooms. This particular room would hold several thousand students without crowding. Democritus himself is at the moment conducting a class. We shall observe that all is silent, since there is no linguistic or vocabulistic sounds which might be interpreted as the consonants of the voice; in other words, he does not talk; as you see instead the instruction is carried on strictly in the process called mental telepathy, a method used entirely in these centers. The mind simply takes the place of the vocal cords, and functions just as does your radio; simple is it not? I would dare to venture a prophecy that before too many hundreds of years a great deal of your communication of the earth will be through just such mental telepathy, as it is called.

Now, as far as I am personally concerned, I do not claim to be a master or even an adept; I am merely an initiate who is attempting in some way to traverse these celestial pathways and adapt my own pathway of life into such fields of endeavor as may be more suitable to a futuristic expression and service in the universal brotherhood. You may question the fact, as did Anton Leeuwenhoek, that although we primarily expressed a relationship in the sciences of optics on the earth, we would not be relegated to such expressions here in the celestial dimensions. As was explained to you, there is science in everything we do, and we are not necessarily confined into the strict channel of our own personal earthy endeavors as we expressed in our previous incarnations. Science is an integrated factor which conceives that each personal endeavor, as it is individualized by every man or woman, becomes scientific in direct degree or relationship or proportion to that in which he best achieves his effort. Even the housewife who is cooking in the kitchen expresses a great deal of science, as you can easily see, in the composition of the various dishes, such as the herbs and spices which go into the cooking pot in a correct balance to enhance the flavor; or as she bakes a loaf of bread which is raised by the process of tiny microorganisms known as yeast cells. This in itself is a scientific and a, 'laboratory' process. You can also see that a painter or any type of craftsman, as has previously been explained to you, indulges and expresses a great deal of science in whatever he does. However, this, as I see, is somewhat repetitious; so I shall go on into a rather descriptive concept, since you have posed the question in your mind as to how and why the buildings, such as you see them, have been so constructed into the various centers and planes in the celestial dimensions.

Before I go into this discussion, however, may I say that Anton was somewhat discomfited, when he reviewed his rather lengthy discourse, to see that he had completely omitted the mention of some of his most famous countrymen, or those who were associated in the immediate vicinity of Holland or Belgium. I am referring to the artistic concept of painting. He did not mention his very worthy countrymen, Van Dyke, Rembrandt or some of the other very famous artists who were closely associated to the country of Holland. Rubens and Rembrandt were two who were quite well known and who have survived the ages of time. I wish you could explore your history books if you are not familiar with the full impact of this memorable age of Reformation, so that you might better acquaint yourself with the great number of very advanced and illumined minds which reincarnated into the earth plane at that period of its evolution.

Now, as you have been visiting these centers you have failed to see some of the familiar sights which you might associate with some of the large earth cities, such as gangs of men who would be repairing streets or craftsmen who might also be repairing the public buildings. There is no necessity for such maintenance work here in these large cities, for these buildings were primarily constructed of the mind forces and energies; and they are further nourished and perpetuated into the posterity of time by mere usage; otherwise, they would of course very quickly be absorbed back into the radiant energy dimension from whence they sprang if they were not constantly kept alive, vibrant and pulsating with the love, the care, and the adoration by the multitudes who pass in and out of these doorways of these different edifices. In other words, nothing is useless in God's world and there is a constant changing of these great cyclic patterns which you call time and space.

Living on the earth as I did at my period of time, I made the same common mistakes as many of the physicists and other men of science are still making in your time; I tried to derive all my equations and formulas from that particular third plane dimension. Of course, it just didn't work. I have had to learn, since coming here, to discard most of these concepts and to start afresh from entirely different directions to assimilate and to formulate conceived patterns of philosophy and science.

Now that you better understand the formulation or the building of some earthly structure which is of benefit to mankind in general, let us construct an allegorical equation. We shall say that a very small group of people who are at the present moment conducting some small religious faction or group or church organization on your earth plane has a sincere and earnest desire to build a larger church, the better to serve a future generation and to perpetuate their own spiritual concept; therefore, they begin with earnest prayers and concentration of mental energies. Because these people are all more or less sympathetic in their vibrations, because they exist in the same section of the great void in time and space, and because they adhere closely for the same purpose, the unity of vibration of their energies, called harmonic or frequency relationship, will, in a future day, so concentrate that this unified force will enable the spiritual powers from some of the higher astral centers to use these energies and to direct them into the proper constructive channels whereby the forces will be set in motion for the actual construction of that church.

However, usually the energies in the spiritual dimensions will actually assume the exact configuration of the earth church in the spiritual world before it is ever built in the material world; and it will continue to exist in the spiritual as long as it does in the material world, for it too is nourished and kept living and pulsating and regenerating with the great abundance of the Radiant Energies here in these celestial dimensions. That is the reason for so many of these very beautiful buildings that you see here about you, which seem to be somewhat connected with the more recent periods of history of your earth planet. There are other reasons, too, for the existence of these beautiful celestial mansions, for they have been conceived with the futuristic ideas of the Logi or Lords who were the controlling and dominating minds in conceiving these celestial dimensions for the service of the lower orders of mankind.

There is also another way in which a group of people may construct a church. We shall say that in several of the astral worlds will be large groups of people who will be vibrating in sympathetic union with each other, even though they may be consciously unaware of each other's existence; yet their energies or the propagation of their mind forces are likewise gathered together. Consequently, at some future day, many of these people will reincarnate into the earth plane dimension or into some similar plane; and, using the constructive energies of that celestial church which they have previously conceived in their mind, they will reconstruct this church in their own relative dimension.

Do not confine your concept to churches, however; many other great buildings, libraries, museums, auditoriums, music halls, yes, even skyscrapers are also dreams and preconceived realizations of people in the more celestial or astral dimensions, long before these structures were brought into actual existence in some terrestrial planet. What I have attempted to explain to you at this time is that there is nothing which is happenstance in God's great universal world. The higher the intelligence, the more expressive it becomes; and so it expresses itself in the more relative dimensions beneath it, as useful and constructive purpose for those who are less fortunate and who do not have the mentality which is conducive to achieving the concept of the higher principles of the spiritual universes. It is quite natural that the savage in the jungle could be of little use in serving mankind in a higher stratum or level of your own cultural civilization. So in the spiritual dimensions this is likewise quite true.

I would not attempt to expound any of my physics or mathematics as I learned it on the earth to some of the minds whom I know to be living in celestial dimensions even beyond Parhelion; this would be very foolhardy, since I would be only exhibiting my ignorance. So it must always be that as we achieve a newer or a higher dimension of thought or concept, we must expound and use the principles which we have imbued into our consciousness for the service of those who have not yet traversed into our levels of thought and consciousness. Anton is standing here very close to me, and he wishes to pass to you his very best fondest regards; so it is with him and myself, since we are both very closely connected to your own dimension of thought in your earthly expression. As he said, we were something of godfathers to you; therefore, it is only natural that he, as well as I, would like to give you something of a little more personal nature.

Now just in case that you may think we have arrived at a stalemate here by not being able to get past the Grecian center of arts and culture, we shall continue on in our exploration, and actually see some of the cities and settings which were characteristic of the period of the Reformation. Your own earth at the present time is very rich in the memories of the contributions of the various philosophers, painters, musicians, poets, and scientists, as they were expressed at that time. If you are fortunate enough to be vested with some of the means to travel into some of the European countries, you can also actually see some of the buildings, museums, and dwelling places of some of these very famous illustrious persons who

lived at the time of the Reformation. But for the benefit of teachers and students who come from other
dimensions or other terrestrial planets, and not yet
reincarnated into the earth plane at any time, these
buildings to a large degree have existed and, as I have
explained, still exist in the centers here of Aureleus;
so through one of the centers you could traverse the
great streets and thoroughfares which would be lined
on either side with buildings which I would not take
the time to enumerate. A catalogue or a study of the
history books of the earth of your time will acquaint
you with the various places which exist in France,
Germany, Holland, Italy, England, Spain, and in other
countries where the Reformation took place.

During the time of the last great world holocaust,
World War II, as it is termed, a few of the art treasures were lost to the world; however, it is very fortunate that the dictators who overran Europe at that
time were somewhat penurious in their intent, and
so collected most of the paintings and various other
artistic treasures of the earth; and thus they were
actually saved from the destructive bombings, which
may possibly have destroyed many of them. My own
country, if I can still call Italy my country, was saved
from much of the horrors of this great war. The
familiar tower of Pisa in my home town still stands;
so likewise with the great art treasures of Rome. The
Basilica and the various other great cathedrals and
historical palaces were also saved. So it is indeed
fortunate, as these things existed only on your earth
and relate considerably into the progression of man
in one planetary aspect.

It is quite necessary that personages from other
terrestrial as well as celestial planets and dimensions
are made thoroughly acquainted with the progress
and the evolution of the earth; thereby earth's trea-

sures are thus kept in an intact condition here in Aureleus. You might spend the equivalent of a hundred years of the earth time in strolling up and down the various streets and into the different buildings of this period of the Reformation, since it has been kept intact for posterity and for mankind in his study of spiritual evolution in Aureleus.

A tour of this section here would begin something like one of the travel tours which have been instituted in your earth time at this particular evolution. You might begin with the Louvre of Paris, the great museum, and there see the art treasures and collections of many of the great masters as they appeared in the period of Reformation. You might go from town to town, and in the itinerary of your travel you would go into the different buildings and even visit the dwelling houses of these philosophers and scientists who lived on earth during the Reformation. However, I must say that such a trip, even on your planet earth at this time, would consume many years, as there were numerous exponents of these different arts and sciences during those several hundred years.

If my observation serves me right, it is rather a barren world in which you are living at the present moment. The present generations have not produced the musicians or artists or philosophers or literary geniuses of that Reformation period. Now I know this statement may be challenged by some who are somewhat loyal to some of the exponents of today's arts and sciences; but you need only to consult the pages of history or to listen to the great orchestras or to visit the museums to prove the fallaciousness of such ideas. Yours is a synthetic age, one which is highly streamlined and tailored to the exploitation of the masses. It is not conducive to the more purely inspirational side of man's nature. However, your period of time does also present tremendous contrasts into various interpretations of the inner natures of man. We do see the struggles in the many branches and in the interpretation of the inner natures of man, and in the interpretations of the spiritual ideologies. They are indeed very numerous at your time, and it seems that anyone who is inclined, can go about postulating some new theory, thereby contriving somehow to place himself in the eye of the public. It is very fortunate for the many people of your time that they are living in your age; if they had lived in the time of my sojourn on the earth, they would have suffered a quick and short life indeed for expressing such theories publicly.

I wish sincerely that my anxiety to speak to you this evening did not cause you some discomfiture, as I know that the spiritual vibrations are not the most conducive pattern of relationship; and it may be possible in the future, if you should desire a more perfect transcript, that I shall reappear, just as did Anton, to render further discussions in a more lengthy and possibly a more intelligible pattern of continuity. You will grant me that it is indeed strange to speak in the tongue and in the vernacular of your present day, after not having done so for several hundreds of years; and confronted as I am with the vastness and the infinity of the great celestial universes about me, I am somewhat confounded by the task of properly presenting to you even a small part of that which I can see about me; and having that presentation orientated to the most palatable mental assimilation in the books which are being compounded at the present moment.

The number and variety of subjects and things which could be talked about and visited here, in Aureleus alone, are staggering and beyond the imagination. What we are specifically trying to convey to the individual on the earth dimension is most pertinent and vital to man's development. It is to remove the obstruction which confines man's thinking in the third dimensional world about him, so that he may properly evaluate and conceive the structures and philosophies that may arise, rather than accept the reactionary concepts which exist about these philosophies.

I could enumerate numerous ideologies and philosophies as they have been conceived on the earth at my time; or in the immediate vicinity of that time you would find, just as I or any one else have found, that these ideologies were all very largely contradictory in themselves; as a result, people related their own interpretation to these writings and interpretations. Philosophies are useful only in the relationship that a student makes as he reads, visualizes, and interprets these philosophies, thus enabling the student to properly interpret his own values and philosophical interpretations of life. A student should never at any time try to compound within his own personal philosophies any structures verbatim as they have been laid down by the philosophers of some previous time or age. These teachers in themselves could lead a person in a zig-zag, round about fashion, and he would get absolutely nowhere. The extraction of principles, as they relate to truth in his own progression, is of the utmost importance; yet he should never lose sight of the fact that his perspective or concept of truth changes daily; and with the daily changes, his mentality should be so flexible in nature that his progression is assured to its fullest intent and purpose. So until we meet again, your true friend and brother,

— Galileo.

CHAPTER 61

Salutations, brother and sister; I am an individual of royal French birth, who lived upon the earth in the 1700's. My father was a nobleman. I was then known as Joseph Louis Lagrange, something of a mathematician and a scientist. My time of life on the earth was somewhat later than that of Galileo, who preceded me in a transmission. However, my interest here with you is very similar to his; and so that you will better be able to trace a continuity in our discussion of philosophies in our visitations, I shall explain somewhat the personal nature of my life on the earth at that time. As a mathematician, I was useful in the service of humanity in postulating the theories in the problems of space and time and the concepts which later enabled Einstein to formulate his basic theories of relativity. I also expounded theories which related to the mathematical formulas or principles which were more pertinent to the mechanics of the earth at that period. Isaac Newton had formulated very definite theories in astrophysics and the mechanics of the universe at a somewhat earlier date. I also gave changes in mathematical structures, which gave a common denomination of ten, as opposed to the previously accepted numerical equivalent of twelve. There were also some changes and clarifications of the metric system of measurements, which before my time had been both confusing and puzzling.

Now that I have given you a brief digest of my activities as a scientist upon the earth, we shall go directly into the business of the exploration and the digestion of the various facets of knowledge and wisdom as might best be conceived in our explorations of Aureleus. Until now you have somewhat thoroughly explored the Grecian, the Asian or the Hindu, and I believe too the Egyptian portion of the city. Now we shall ascend to one of the higher points, on one of the towers of a great church here in this city, which is a part of the outer section of the center of the city of Aureleus, so that we may best look out over the city. You will thus be enabled to get a better view of the entire landscape as it is composed, as was described by Galileo, of numerous buildings, churches, museums, and individual dwelling houses of the many thousands of philosophers and various scientists who have lived on earth at different periods of time.

In order to avoid a little confusion in your thinking, we shall say that philosophy is in itself not a pure science, nor is it classified as such. Philosophy can and does assume many individual forms or component parts of the aspects of the life of the individual, as was explained in previous discussions. Now that we are in the observation portion of this great belfry of this large church, I might mention, incidentally, that this church is one of those now in existence in France. Looking out over the city, you will see the various buildings; and since it would take a very long time to pursue the course of the streets and to inspect each building individually, we shall stand here quietly near the rail of this observation balcony and look out over the city while we discuss some more of the relative facets of the philosophies and ideologies as they were conceived on the earth plane at the period of the Renaissance and Reformation.

In my life I lived to see the death throes of the great Holy Roman Empire; and by the time I had passed from the earth, the courts of inquisition were already being banished and outlawed in countries like France, England, and other places where they had previously existed. Spain, however still maintained somewhat of a tyrannical disposition of the inquisition in a form something of a government within a government. But generally speaking, the yoke of tyranny was almost overthrown.

By now I hope that you have formed in your minds something of the various and, may I say, contradictory aspects of the various philosophies. We may begin with the Jewish Dutchman, Spinoza, and his classical philosophies, and those who were somewhat directly opposed to the empirical doctrines of John Locke. We could discuss the monadic concepts of Leibnitz and find it also was somewhat different in many aspects to that of Kant, the German philosopher. Fredrick Jacobi also was violently opposed to many of the concepts which were contained in the philosophies of Immanuel Kant.

Several of the other philosophers who came later attempted to combine the various spiritual and mystical elements of philosophy with those of the more materialistic or empirical doctrines. Swedenborg realized much of the spiritual concept. Spencer, in the late 1800's, however, seemed to combine elements which were so judicially chosen and placed that they presented a more factual and interpretative philosophy of life. Emerson, in his Essays and other works also attempted somewhat to pacify many of the opposing factions in the philosophical realm. Many of the other philosophers whom I could name at this time changed horses in the middle of the stream, if I may use one of the more familiar colloquialisms, which is interpretative in this type of switch in the mental processes of thinking.

Now we do not confine the characteristic elements of the personal philosophies into the realm of the pure philosophical interpretations themselves. We find such individual margins of personal identity contained in the pages of the various poetic works. We can also see in the interpretations of such great artists as Van Dyke, Rembrandt, and Rubens, their own individual personal works of identity. Even the brush strokes themselves are earmarks of the master who created the painting. In the field of music, the compositions, the chords, and the various tonal effects are likewise characteristic of the individual and are such an identification that after some familiarity with music, a person can very easily in a blindfold test immediately identify the compositions as they are being played on the electronic instruments of your time, or in the orchestrations as they have been recorded.

The point which I am making most emphatically is that in the personal correlation of your own interpretation of a philosophy of life, we can rightly assume that the personal philosophies of all of these various thousands of individuals who have lived on the earth plane came into being and passed into the pages of history simply because they were factional in themselves and contained only a small and individualized concept of the great and universal cosmos of truth. Such individuals, just as I myself who passed into what you might call the limbo of the vastness of space into the hinterlands or the spiritual dimensions, do so, not with the assumed authority that we have given so much or so little to the posterity of man, nor that our philosophies are in themselves invaluable or not subject to change. We in ourselves realize the insufficiency of such ideologies; and the new dimensions and in the new expressions into which we have evolved, we come to realize the insufficiency of such ideologies and philosophies. I would not have these words be misconstrued to belittle the personal efforts of those who have worked and striven and spent a lifetime in the expression of such formulative concepts of life. But only in the pursuance of evaluation of these concepts, do we as individuals avoid some of the pitfalls and mistakes; thus we can extract the elements of philosophies which are most useful to use. Consequently, we can use these elements as stepping-stones in our personal evolution.

However, do not assume at any time that you shall ever come to the time or place when one philosophy will suffice. It suffices only for one evolution. One of the greatest and the richest elements of my own personal progression into the spiritual dimensions was that I had been somewhat of a mathematician on the earth; and thus I was in a most receptive position to absorb the knowledge and wisdom which was so much about me. I found that there seemed to be some great Universal Mind here in these spiritual dimensions. It was not a personal mind, but instead a relative thing which through the law of harmonic relationship, automatically relegated and regulated each individual into his own proper sphere and dimension.

We could say that such a man as Einstein, who recently passed from your earth life into the pages of history, could not immediately ascend into the dimensions of the city of Parhelion, which is devoted to mathematics and sciences. Rather he would become acclimated to a certain degree in some of the lower orders of astral realms or dimensions, which would best enable him further to make his ascension into

Aureleus, or more directly into Parhelion itself.

I never cease to be amazed at the regular procession of cyclic paths of determination and values as they are expressed in these spiritual dimensions; for there are no officials who direct you or who say that you must go to such and such a place, or that it is mandatory that you express yourself in any specific way. A person makes his adjustment automatically and with the greatest of ease in the direction in which he is of the greatest service, and one in which he can best understand the motivating principles of the dimension in which he finds himself.

One of the very interesting facets which I expressed in my earth life was in the study of the various laws of harmonics and its cyclic paths of relationship, such harmonic relationship as is expressed in the twanging or the plucking of strings in the orchestrated instruments. I found that strings had a basic or a fundamental frequency, as I termed this, not only in themselves, but that they also generated and regenerated these frequencies in direct multiples or proportions, which often reached fantastic proportions. I also found that the elimination of any of these harmonics changed the overtone of the string as it was plucked. You may best distinguish this difference to your own advantage by listening to one of the earlier versions of the piano, then called a harpsichord, and then to your modern piano. The difference here is that your modern piano has very thoroughly and effectively damped strings. By damping I do not mean the use of water, but rather the use of small felt pads which are placed near the end of the strings on the string board, which is underneath the framework of the piano itself. These felt pads automatically eliminate the higher wave train frequencies and thus change the overtone of the struck string to such an extent that the piano is an entirely different instrument. I also discovered the interesting phenomenon that two strings, when tuned in portions of octaves, would, when plucked simultaneously, produce a third harmonic structure, which, in the terminology of the physicist of your day, is termed a heterodyne. It is the principle by which the modern radio is tuned and thus is able to assimilate the various frequencies from the air, as they are passed from the transmitters.

Now this, of course, may be somewhat confusing to the untrained mind which has not had some basic knowledge in the field of electronics; however, I am discussing the facts to show you that everything is law, order, and harmony in God's great celestial Universe. Nowhere except in the terrestrial planes such as the earth do we see such an abundance of inharmony and confusion; yet all that may abundantly and superficially appear to be great confusion is actually the beginning of the more basic and elemental forms of the laws of harmonic structures which will separate and regulate each individual into his own proper dimension. This of course comes with the first step of each individual who becomes an initiate. In a sense he becomes his own judge and his own jury by determining what it is that he shall do to direct his mind and his energies into his intents, so that in future evolutions of his life he will automatically ascend and re-ascend into the different dimensions which are more suitable to a higher expression of those concepts; and so, as a humble mathematician, may I give the strongest and most emphatic emphasis to your personal philosophy: it must include the concepts which explain the laws of the higher orders of cyclic motions. Faraday explained to some extent the formation of the suns and the various planets in the solar systems by the vortexes. Such law and order in the more constructive realms is also more or less displayed in all things about us. The law of vibronics and cyclic motion is in itself the fundamental concept of the great Intelligence which is called God, on the earth.

There was at one time an individual living on the earth named Calvin. It was he who formed one of the basic churches still in existence there. The Calvinistic religious influence includes the concept of predestination and various other concepts which regulate the individual to a philosophy of hell-fire and damnation. Such philosophy can or cannot be assimilated or rejected by the individual. He determines his own philosophy by the ability to think factually and constructively for himself; he must learn that such elements in a personal philosophy are widely diversified. Even in your own day you see that the elements of philosophy as expressed among the various Christian factions in your own country are extremely wide and diversified; and they all seem to say that the road to heaven can be entered only through their own doorway.

Now we here know what the doorway is; the doorways into the Celestial Kingdom, if you would call them such, are not through the portals of any one's church, but through the portals of one's own mind. As was previously explained in one of the earlier transmissions from the planet Venus, it all hinges upon the individual's ability to form what is called a concept. Even the most mechanical and mundane processes of our daily life would become absolutely impossible unless we had learned through the reactionary processes of the objective and subconscious mind to manipulate these mechanical processes in our every-day life. Even the act of walking across the room would be an impossibility unless we had so preconditioned our mind into these concepts which move and motivate the various muscles of the mechanism known as the human body. So, ascending into the spiritual dimensions which separate man from this structure of flesh and bone, we do so on the premise that the mind must be so conditioned that it can accept the spiritual concepts which will place it in the direct line of continuity with such dimensions as are most suitable to our own individuality.

Again, a very emphatic statement that I must make is that there is absolutely nothing, and may I repeat, *nothing* which you can conceive in your minds at this day, and far beyond the limits which you can conceive even into the future of many thousands of years, which is not still entirely possible and does not exist in the mind of the great universal cosmos, which is the ultimate and destiny of all mankind in the evolution; and in order to enter into these higher spiritual dimensions, each one must follow the logical pattern of thought of a change in concepts. So whatever it is that you have conceived in your earth philosophies, you will begin to understand that such philosophies would be less than useless in such dimensions and in such realms.

After your many hundreds of thousands of years of evolutions, putting it into the equivalent of earth time, you will have conceived concepts in your mind which would defy description, and would cause you to be completely frustrated in your attempts to find any cohesive relationship with your present earth life; and you would even be unable to picture one small fragment of the evolutions in these future dimensions. You have already seen in a former exploration one of the higher of the Lords or Logi, called Serapis, who was known and lived on the earth at one time. In that presentation he appeared as a living lambent flame of energy, in which he functioned entirely without the customary arms and legs or the organism of the body; and even this, my brother, is only the beginning of the evolutions into which Serapis will yet evolve in his progression into the still higher dimensions.

But I must not confuse you; I must confine myself to channels which are more acceptable to the world in which you live. So, let us rest and mentally digest what we have witnessed and what we have discussed. Your friend,

— Joseph.

CHAPTER 62

This is your humble servant, Lao-Tzu, and it is a most happy occasion that I can be with you again. I see that you are somewhat surprised to find yourself standing in a Chinese temple before a huge statue of Buddha. It is very similar to one which is in China at your particular time. During the past several visitations to Aureleus, you have been led by some of my very worthy brothers who lived in the more recent time in the earth's history. The period of time called the Reformation was very closely connected with your own life on the earth plane. It is hoped by now you and your fellow students have some idea of what has been given you; of what is meant by philosophy, since these transmissions started in the pre-Christian era, in the ancient time of Greece and into the more remote times of India, Egypt, and other great civilizations of the past.

Now it is quite obvious, if you will very earnestly search your histories, that we have mentioned but a very small number of those very illumined persons who have lived on the earth and have contributed to the wisdom of life for the betterment of mankind. However, I do believe that those who have been mentioned and presented to you have, in their own way and in their own capacity, envisioned much of the thinking processes called philosophy or ideologies in the various transitions of life and in the various periods of cycles of history upon the earth.

We cannot neglect the importance of any of these philosophies even though it was very thoroughly emphasized that no one should interpret a philosophy as the ultimate destiny of thinking in the evolution, not only of his own consciousness, but in the minds of his fellow beings. Just as Plato in his philosophy emphasized emphatically that concept was all important and, as he put it, one must understand the dogmas; all of us must also understand the various concepts in all of the things about us so that in the complete envisionment of these concepts, we begin to become more acquainted with the creative processes which are stimulated by the enthusiasm which enters into the conceptive processes.

Socrates was the teacher of Plato who likewise taught Aristotle, the founder of some theories which were later disproved by Galileo. We might say that Pythagoras established numerical or mathematical formulas, which were the basis of the mathematical fields of Newton, Galileo, Legrange, and others of that time and era and, incidentally, leading into the time of your own era of Einstein and others. So we begin to see here in this field alone a very definite relationship in the progress of evolution, or a path or a cycle; neither can we neglect other fundamental relationships which definitely align the progress in evolution of man's consciousness in other fields.

Literature, art, music, and drama, also progressed mightily during the age of the Reformation. The Greek culture including drama, is a classic in history and has in no wise been duplicated since that time. Nevertheless, we cannot neglect the concepts of the Elizabethan era, in which the concepts of the very notable Shakespeare and many others were brought into the focus of public attention. Here again a complete schism in the thinking of the people of that era was brought into a forward and progressive movement. Spontaneously with all of this, was the forward evolution in the field of painting, sculpturing, and other factors which related man to his environment on earth. Even Charles Darwin, expounder of the theory of evolution and progress of mankind as physical beings, is at the present time teaching in one of the astral worlds and is engaged in a vast amount of research. I might say, by the way, that it would be very inconvenient at this time for him to make a transmission.

Getting back to our subject, I can say that all in all, the presentation of the various philosophies, whether they relate to sculpture, art, literature, philosophy, mathematics, or any other field of endeavor, had a very definite relationship to the liberation and the thinking of the progressive evolution of man's consciousness. Man's thinking had been so completely degraded by the imperialistic dogmas of the Holy Roman Empire, in which there was so much abject misery and suffering among the poorer classes; so much opulence and wealth among the wealthy, so many ecclesiastical orders, that the over-balance in the cultural and social natures of men and women of that era was quite necessarily of such tenuity that it had to be completely readjusted and rectified.

Actually as was given to Swedenborg, the complete adjustment and passing of the era transpired at about the middle of the seventeenth century. So you will see, in the tracing of your history, that about the eighteenth century we see the passing of the Holy Roman Empire, the abolition of the courts of the inquisition, and the outlawing of those factional orders of jurisdiction in such countries as France, Sweden, and England. Now, let us get into your present time; but before I do so, may I mention that there is one here among us called Dr. William James who would like, if it is convenient, to conduct a transmission in the future. I might add, casually, that James and Blavatsky have one thing in common: they sometimes very jokingly moan to themselves, "If only I had a good cigar!"

James, as you know, expounded his theory of pragmatism, although he claimed to be an empiricist of the first degree. He was also the founder or exponent of some of the more basic psychological concepts as related to the physiology of mankind on the earth plane at the turn of the nineteenth century.

Next I would like to come to a subject which is a little closer to my heart and which is of a more spiritual philosophy of man's nature; and yet we might say that the spiritual expressions of man in the various evolutions and histories of the world have, in themselves, always presented something of a paradox, inasmuch as they seem always to be confused with man's material nature. However, this is understandable in view of the reactionary philosophy of life into which most individuals enter at the time of their birth. We say each individual enters this Philosophy with such a strongly developed sense of personality that along with the reactionary philosophy of his brothers, sisters, parents, and those of the world about him, all further crystallize and enlarge these concepts of his own personal ego-sense consciousness. It is very difficult for the average person in such a reactionary state of consciousness to separate himself from his self, to envision or enlarge his horizon sufficiently to the point where spiritual aspects in their proper relationship truly enter into his consciousness. Thus, in his early as well as in his later expressions of spiritual philosophy, he has confounded and confused the Deistic Beings, or as he might call them, gods or demons or the various other factions or powers which he can envision, who lived in an enlightened or a superstructure of spiritual dimension.

The more primitive and ancient man pictured gods riding in the thunderclouds; the sun, a huge god who rained its heat and light upon the earth; the mountains, the hills, and the rocks inhabited and frequented by such spirits of the earth, air, fire, and water. We find concepts of such nature still existing even down into the more modern times, such as druidism and the various Greek and Roman pantheons, that have existed and still exist in the more inaccessible reaches of some of the countries of Greece and Italy. However, in all cases we find that the controlling and dominating factor, as expressed in the deistic concept of the being who rules the destiny of man in that particular expression, is personified as an individual.

In your modern Christian theologies, most people who attend the Christian churches do so with the belief that they cannot envision God as anything except a super being who rules in some celestial palace, sitting on a throne, writing everyone's name in a huge book, and making little x's or o's after each name denoting the temperament or disposition of the individual. Such is the Judgment Day of some far-off time, as written in the Book of Peter in which He shall come as a thief in the night. Why would God come as a thief in the night? Why should He destroy one of His planets with a rain of fire and burn all things from the surface? Such a philosophy and such a prediction is in contradiction to the simple philosophy which was taught by Jesus who, in his own way, taught the all-forgiving, the loving, the everlasting presence of God within all things. In my most ancient China, we find even to this day, groups or individuals who shave all but a small piece on the top of the head where their hair grows out into a long queue by means of which they believe they shall be snatched into heaven by some unseen hand. We find a similarity in the Christian philosophy, in which the blood of Jesus and the belief in Him will guarantee salvation even for the blackest and most vile sinner should he call upon the name of this personage.

It is small wonder that there is little progress in the Christian churches where such contradictory philosophies are preached and where each minister or priest, in his own way, expounds his own theories and concepts. However, there is a universal appeal in the belief that the blood of Jesus will wash away sins. My friends, your sins are very necessary in the experiences of your life, for they are the determining factors of your evolutionary progress. You are on the earth at this time to understand the difference between earth's experiences whether they are good or detrimental to your own progress. How else would you be able to determine right from wrong if all were good or all were evil? It would be very difficult, I assure you.

There are other very seeming contradictions in the Christian Philosophies, just as there are in the other spiritual philosophies which exist among the peoples of the world. In the case of the Christian religion it is much more so; because, if we understand the origin and the founding of the Christian churches, which became the Holy Roman Empire, we shall see that compounds of cults, as they exist in the Mithraic concepts, are interwoven with and are in direct contradiction to the simple elemental faith and manifestation of the inward spiritual consciousness as was taught by Jesus. So the great Roman Catholic Church sprang into existence and has now become somewhat the pattern for all churches; inasmuch as the lavishness and the garishness of the edifices of these churches, with their golden altars, their beautiful rugs, their carved marble statues, their wealth, and the possessive materialism which surrounds these great churches, are themselves in direct contradiction to the rock on which Jesus stood and preached the Beatitudes. I shall not attempt at this time to under-rate in a spiritual sense the values of the churches or the Christian philosophy as it exists in your country today. Such blind and obstructed faith is much better than nothing; as a lame man with a broken leg must walk with a crutch, so the Christian who is unable to think constructively for himself, must lean upon the lame philosophies as they are expounded from the very un-Christian churches of the world.

As Karl Marx expressed himself, (and I would not say that I am communistic; it would make little difference if you called me communistic, because I am in a place where the word means nothing) any philosophy or religion which subtracts the individual self-consciousness from the true perspective of realism, such realistic separations will, in themselves, tend to subjugate the individual to such low planes of mental atrophy as to completely stop his spiritual evolution. So it is, in the belief that anyone can save us from our sins. We must first conceive sin or error as that which is sin only if we let it remain as such in our consciousness. Most everyone on the earth has some guilt complex, compounded from the multiplicity of sins, as they are called in the earth dimension. The existence of these things in themselves are relatively inconsequential. They mean little or nothing. The most important element in the undergoing of such sinful experiences is that it leaves the individual with a resolution that he has now determined the factional difference between right and wrong and that he must work toward a better end. No one can do this for him. It is his own will; it is his own dominion, and his own life.

Jesus would be defeating the purpose of his mission on earth if He had left behind the word that He had come to "*save*" the world. The obvious fact remains that the Christians have confused the word Jesus with Christ. Now, to further analyze constructively what is meant by Jesus and the Christ: in the Christian churches, the two words are used almost simultaneously and are usually believed to be the name of an individual, just as I am Lao-Tzu. Such is not the case. Let us refer back to our original concept that God is Infinite in His nature, and in order to be Infinite, He must also express Himself into many finite dimensions. The Infinity of God in so expressing Himself to the individual comes into the individual's consciousness from the Superconscious state of the individual's own personal structure. We say, therefore, that God assumes and radiates Himself into the personage of the individual as a person because, as I have previously stated in the philosophy of man, man in his earth life is an individual and undergoes the very strong association of personal ego consciousness with himself to all deistic influences.

Therefore God in man as an individual must become the Christ, and that Christ is God. It was thus explained by Jesus when he stated, "The Father and I are one and the same." Is that not so? So it is with all of you; you must personify God as Christ, the living embodiment of all things which you yourself crave, hope and desire to be; your most innate nature as you have sprung from the Divine Fountainhead, which is God. Thus you must revert into the complete attunement of such consciousness. Before doing so, as has been explained, you evolve through many dimensions, through many lifetimes; and in so doing, you achieve the finite understanding of all consciousness. This you have called sin and error. In associating yourselves with the lower materialistic elements of the lowest of the elemental planes of understanding in God's great Mind, you have thus undergone the experience of sin and error in your evolutions through what you call space and time, or reincarnation. Thus you develop in your consciousness the personified being of Christ, and thus it is with each individual. I hope that I have made myself clear.

Therefore, in the future, my dear ones, it would be well for each of you to mark today as a distinct birthday in the history of your personal development and evolution. The day will be when you separate yourself from the blood concept. The blood and stench of the slaughterhouse should not mingle with the pure incense of God's pure Divine Love. It is not understandable to us here that the highest precepts of spiritual consciousness should be founded upon the transgressions of man upon another man, or that such Christian concepts should be exploited to their fullest attainment with the usage at the display of some man who had been crucified by his fellowman. It would be well for these churches to submerge their consciousness into some other expression and teach differently. The philosophy of Christianity could thus be more easily understood by the more simple and primitive thinking people of the world, who have not so confounded their minds with civilization.

In the future it would be well too for the Christian churches if they would teach a more practical philosophy of life; if they would learn to understand the true innermost nature of mankind; if they would learn to understand the spiritual motivations and

516

principles which inspired the Beatitudes and the teachings and the psychological principles which were behind the words spoken by Jesus. We do not confound the man Jesus with the Christ, because Christ is the distinct separation of a dimension and not an individual. Christ, as I said, is the personification of God into each individual; and I might add a word, that the descent of Christ, as he has promised in some future day, will not be as an individual. What Jesus meant was that the Christ, the spiritual God, would come unto the earth and infuse the minds and hearts of all individuals, so that they would live more constructively, more spiritually, and they would love their fellowman; but until such day, may I remain your most humble servant.

Now that we have made adjustments, may I speak a little more please. I believe I was talking about the progression of the individual through the various material planes of existence and about his acquiring such materialistic philosophies and knowledge as pertained to these dimensions, which will enable him to progress further in his evolution into the higher spiritual domains. In order that my remarks may not be misconstrued or erroneously interpreted, I do not advocate that a person should purposely set out to undergo sinful experiences with the idea in mind that such experiences will further advance his spiritual growth. Such is not the case. The determining element is what you think is sin or error. We say that the ordinary experiences in the material world are, in themselves, largely sinful. There are many things about you in your earth life which lead to guilt complexes. We could say that things which induce such complexes are sinful in nature. Because of the complexity in a concept of the food which mankind eats, one man says eat flesh; another says abstain and eat

517

nothing but vegetables; others say this is good or that is not so good. As a result, you yourself become confused and you believe that your stomach is constantly upset by what you do eat. Consequently, you have a neurosis and you have suffered sin. We might say that the association of man and woman in the field called sex is also conducive of a great number of guilt complexes and neuroses. Each person has his own concept in regard to his conduct in the relationship of sex. No two people seem to be able to agree on one or more points in their own individual translations. The various conflicts in this field give rise to some of the greatest and most deep rooted of the guilt complexes of human nature.

Now, it is sinful if a person indulges in some heinous crime, such as murder or robbery. This is perversion. It is perversion of the principle of the Intelligent God Force which created the individual. It is not purely sin, but is something which needs a stronger word than sin. So my classification of sin relegates mankind into the more simple and natural experiences of his existence, because in his life on the earth plane, he has no criteria to determine which is sin and error. As a result, he is constantly confounding himself in his daily life by listening to the prattle of his fellow men in regard to what they consider their interpretations of good and evil. Therefore, man has so imbued into his subconscious mind the conflicts of the various natures of the individuals about him that he becomes neurotic and extremely activated in his subconscious mind with the conflicts of guilt complexes, with the thought that this is sin and that is error. Any of the earth philosophies or any of the spiritual philosophies, for that matter, which give rise to dissatisfaction, unrest, unhappiness, or even physical disease in the body of a human being is,

518

in itself a sinful practice.

One does not necessarily need to commit an act in a physical sense to commit a sin; to think murder or to inflict harm in some way on one's fellow man, even though it is done mentally, is just as evil and sinful as if it were done in a physical way. After all, it is merely the absolute concept of what takes place in the individual's mind. It is the obsessive realism of such an act of violence, an act of crime, which takes place in the individual's mind; whether he actually carries this through in a physical sense is of secondary importance. Therefore one must refrain from any destructive tendencies, any perversions of mentality which might detour him from his true path of evolution; he must not be concerned with the translations of what is sin and error by his fellow man. No one is so absolute in judgment, in wisdom, or in knowledge, to determine what is sinful and erroneous in the conduct of another's daily life.

This decision is a determining factor in your own consciousness. You may call it the still small voice as was previously given, but whatever you call it, it is the Superconsciousness, the combined voices of your Guardian Angels and of those who are associated with you in your spiritual dimensions. It can also be the voice of the vortexes from your psychic body which speak through the consciousness of your objective mind, and which will in some strange vague way warn you to deter from perversions of mentality. So long as you listen to these warnings, so long as you take the absolute stand that you are progressing spiritually and that you must always retain the consciousness of that motivating vital spiritual voice within the Superconsciousness as long as you realize that you are connected through the Christ Force within you to the Central Vortexes of God's own Infinite Nature, then, my brothers, you cannot detour far from the true path of progression.

There is much more I would like to discuss with you; however, in looking over my remarks to you in these past few moments I believe I left nothing which can be falsely misconstrued. So, for the present, we shall return to our respective dimensions and seek our own life. Your true friend and brother,

— Lao-Tzu.

CHAPTER 63

This is Gamaliel; I was standing by listening to Lao-Tzu and his very fine discussion on some of the principles of Christianity on your earth plane. I do believe that the subject is very broad in all its facets and concepts, as it is related directly or indirectly with the concepts of many other religious philosophies which are, and have been, in existence on the earth for hundreds of thousands of centuries. It might be well to discuss further the concept of the Christ and of the personal relationship of man with the Christ consciousness within himself.

We can begin first by drawing something of an allegory; we say a man lives in a house; therefore, we say that the man *is* the house; because a man is living in a body, the body is the man. In your Christian Bible you begin with the concept of the beginning of man. God gathered up the dust of the earth, formed a body, and breathed the breath of life into him and he became man. This is a parable, but strangely enough, it is almost factual. We see on your earth plane, as on other worlds of such nature, the growing things of the earth in their productiveness, become the foods and the elements of sustenance to the animals which exist in these worlds. Man feeds upon the animals and the plants. Since the body is constantly being reconstructed and rebuilt, is not man therefore built of the elements of the earth and *of* the *earth itself?* Only the added elements of sunshine and of the aerobic contents of the air about him enter into the construction and become the catalytic agents which are combined with the life forces which stem from the psychic body.

However, the body should not in any way be confused with the man. The man exists in direct association with the body, or he is within the body, just as the man is within the house. The body is merely a mechanism, a bony structure, over which is stretched various muscles, compounded to form levers and fulcrums, which motivate the various structural forms of the limbs, hands, arms, legs, and feet, to enable man to have locomotion. He has lungs to breathe the gas from the atmospheric envelope which surrounds the earth, and which enters into the compound metabolistic processes which carry on the force within the body. But what is the motivating force behind the life force? There again is the psychic body, which links itself to the Superconsciousness of the individual himself.

The individual is the Christ, the Christ within everyone. It is this Christ, and the belief in and the knowledge of this Christ, which saves all men from the iniquities keeping them in the lower levels of physical expression. So does not Christ save each man? But only the consciousness, the knowledge, and the wisdom *of this Christ* will enable the individual to work with this Christ Consciousness. This Christ Consciousness is in itself a part of the intelligence of man which links him directly with the great God Force. If you study the histories of the seven great Avatars who have lived on your earth plane, you may ask if all of them are not Jesus, or are all of them not the Christ? Yes, indeed they are all the Christ in the simple way in which I have explained this concept to you; for they are individualized personifications or individual Christs. They have merely attained in their spiritual development, a more conscious workable continuity of consciousness within them; as a result, they have become Christ-like in their being and in their expression.

In traveling through the various evolutions or reincarnations, and rising in the processes whereby you are initiated into these various spiritual concepts, you begin more and more to be a person of two beings. You are overshadowed by the Superconsciousness, as was true of the Man of Galilee whom you call Jesus. He was so overshadowed by His Consciousness, His Christ Self, that this continuity of thought and structure in the philosophy of His life enabled Him to perform the many miracles, because it linked Him immediately with the great God Force.

Is this explanation not better than to believe, as does the man who sits on a pile of brick, that if he sits long enough his house will be built for him? We might tell the story of the man who lived in the house with the leaky roof; the traveler who passed by when it was raining asked the man why he did not fix his roof. He answered, "I can't; it is raining." Later when the sun was shining, the passing traveler again asked the man why he did not fix his roof. His reply then was that there was no need since the sun was shining. Thus it is with people in their spiritual philosophies. They are constantly procrastinating for one reason or another. They must be led by those who would so exploit their weaknesses, that they are led into false channels which subject them to the opiates of procrastination, the self indulgences of philosophies whereby someone else can do it for them and thus they have no need to do it; all they have to do is to believe. This philosophy *is not true,* my friends. In your spiritual evolution you will progress only by the conscious continuity and understanding of the principle of the Christ-Consciousness; the individualized personification of God, which acts in the uppermost reaches and thus, in an indirect way, into the conscious or the objective mind of every individual. Peace be with you,

— Gamaliel.

CHAPTER 64

Good evening, children; this is a different situation from any in which I have been before. I am standing here, and yet I am not standing here; and, as you no doubt can smell, I am smoking one of my Corona-Corona cigars. Now, Dr. Pearce and I have been standing by from time to time to watch the procession as some of the teachers and initiates here come through to talk to you, and note how you take it all down, and indeed it is very interesting. So I thought I would take a whack at it myself. Now this business of philosophy; you no doubt have read something about my activities on the earth about forty-five or fifty years ago; it may be a little longer than that; time gets away from you up here. I was interested in philosophy and psychology, and as a doctor, I fiddled around a little with the human body. However since coming here, I have managed to learn much that would have been very valuable to me on the earth plane. I have noticed in the various transmissions, as they are called, numerous references made to some of the Grecian philosophers as well as to some of the comparatively more recent or modern ones, who lived during the Middle Ages or period of Reformation; and they all seemed to call themselves something or another, or at least they called their philosophy by some particular name.

We say that John Locke called himself an Empiricist and because I was very interested in Locke at one time I called myself an Empiricist also until I adopted a philosophy of my own. Then Dr. Pearce called me a Pragmatist, so I really don't know what I am at the present moment. I have been studying and learning many things about which the earth doctors and philosophers know little or nothing. In studying here and in keeping up with the times of the earth as things go on down there with you now, one thing I know for certain; and that is you are living in an age of specialization. If a man is a doctor, he specializes on one particular part of the anatomy. For example, even if a man is an automobile mechanic, he specializes on carburetors; as a result, if one should get caught on the road with a mechanic who did not know anything but carburetors, they would be in difficulty if something were to go wrong with the back end of the automobile. Now I don't know whether this system is right or whether it is not. I think that everyone should know a great deal about whatever he is doing, especially in the world of medicine in relation to the elements of human life, and in an understanding of whatever principles are involved in the continuance of life.

So it is with the psychiatrist, a pet subject of mine. I have found in studying the numerous types of psychiatry, as they are brought into being and practiced in your world of today, that they all have one universal fault, with hardly an exception. They take little or no cognizance of the fact that man is a spiritual creature, first, last and always. They seem to think that a person is a mass of muscle and bone and that the body is in some strange way activated or motivated by the impulses from the various portions of the brain. When one comes to analyze their concept about the subconscious, about which they talk much, none of them seems to know just exactly what the subconscious is. They believe that it is something and that it is somewhere, but they do not know what it is. Of course you have been told numerous times in these transmissions that the subconscious consists of countless tiny wiggly wave forms which go to make up the person's spiritual or psychic body, and that is quite true. The various vortexes contained within this psychic body are constantly in revolution around their vortexes. They are manifesting and repeating the same thought patterns which originally motivated or brought into being the vortrocentric forces of these tiny vortexes. They are called by the modern psychiatrist inhibitions or neuroses, depending upon their size or intensity; but you will have a difficult time proving that point to some of these wise boys on the earth in your time. They must have something they can see or on which they put their hands or which they can tap with a little mallet. So I really don't know how you will go about that; they will just have to learn the hard way, I suppose.

Now, in the field of philosophy, man is essentially a spiritual creature and is composed of such spiritual counterparts of himself as exist in different dimensions, for man does not exist on the earth plane all by himself and all alone. Through his psychic body, he is linked and relinked with the numerous other dimensions and with the various types and kinds of vibrations which go on about him in this plane. More than that, however, is the fact that he has a Superconscious being which links him still further into the higher dimensions. We might say that this Superconscious self is the complete embodiment of all that he is, minus his other polarity, or, as you have been taught, the biocentric counterpart of himself.

Of course, the psychiatrists of your time know nothing of these spiritual elements and facts entering into the makeup of the individual; and for that reason so many of them have so little success with the mental problems which seem to be multiplying, and the rate of insanity and mental aberrations which are continually mounting. The asylums in your time are filled to overflowing. Although the psychiatrist can treat only the condition which seems to him to come from the normal processes of life, yet he calls his treatment of these normal processes of living psychosomatic medicine. Now that is true so far as it goes; a person can incur many types of inhibitive neuroses in the progressive cycles of years in the daily manipulative processes of his ordinary life. But more than that, every individual (as we have said) keeps coming into these earth plane dimensions, Heaven only knows how many times; evolving again and again in those material dimensions and seems to be getting nowhere at all.

It matters not what you call the various kinds of mental aberrations from which people suffer. I could name off several hundred, which would mean little or nothing to the average individual. As the list would only occupy space and cause Ruth much typing, I shall present my little discussion in a more intelligible fashion that will mean more to more people. In my association on the earth I was very close to my very dear friend Dr. Pearce, who was quite an authority and knew considerably about conditions known as obsessions. This topic also happens to be one which is not only completely ignored, but vilified; and anyone who believes in obsessions or the adherence of evil spirits to a personality is considered a quack, an individual whose efforts are spurious and should be completely ignored, or better still, he should be countermanded to some mental institution. Nevertheless, these things do exist; they have always existed in the histories of man upon whatever earth plane he is found. In fact, you may even find obsessions existing in some of the higher astral worlds. Some of us here in the centers of Shamballa know too well that we are not entirely immune from the obsessive effects or the possibilities of incurring some attachments, if we venture into the astral dimensions which are inhabited by these lower and less advanced types of humanity. So wherever you are over here, it at least pays to be a little careful, just as it does over there. I would venture to say that possibly 90% of the inmates of the institutions in your countries have complications involving obsessive characteristics which are impounded from the direct influence of astral entities or retrograde personalities, who have gone down into the lower dimensions—the basement, if you will call it such—the places where these negative entities seem to go.

It is not because there are such places. It is simply because people do not take advantage of their time; they fail to study and to learn to commune with their inner self and to learn what the spiritual nature of man is, and where he will go when he leaves the earth. People are too busy indulging themselves in material values of the world about them. They may be too interested in some woman, or the woman too interested in some man. You know the story as well as I do. The result is that when they lose their little temple of flesh, they find themselves unequipped. They are in a strange world of which they know nothing; and the result is that they are in a very unfortunate predicament. Of course, many of them are helped and we know the history. Any one who is on the pathway of Truth knows considerably about what takes place when the individual goes into the spiritual dimensions. I remember my own experience quite well and when I lost my little temple, I was not quite aware of the fact for some time. Things seemed to go on much the same way as they did before until one day someone came along and tapped me on the shoulder and said; "You're dead." So I looked around and sure enough, I was; but that is the way it is over here sometimes.

In regard to obsessions and exorcism, I would like to see, and I believe I shall if I stay around the centers here in Shamballa long enough, the day when it will be generally conceded that there will be a swing-back into the concepts which will enable the psychiatrist to use various methods, such as hypnotism and other methods known to the more ancient peoples. The Egyptians had a very highly developed art of psychiatry which involved exorcism. There are many other races of people on the earth who have been equally enlightened for many hundreds of thousands of years (and still are, for that matter) and are today casting out evil spirits. Of course, because we see the retrograde examples of exorcism, we have more or less tossed the whole idea in the basket, the inferior with the superior methods, and considered them all inferior and therefore eliminated them from psychiatry. All that will have to be relearned. In my day on the earth considerable attention was paid to the possibility that the person could be obsessed by some entity from some dimension. In fact, if we read the histories of the New England States, in the beginning many people were accused of having obsessions and were taken out and burned at the stake. In fact, down through the Middle Ages many people, especially a woman who gave birth to a deformed infant, would be accused of consorting with an incubus. An incubus was a devil who had fornicated with a woman during the night in her sleep; and so she was burned.

Your modern psychiatrists all have a tendency to pooh-pooh these ideas and throw up their hands and say "old wives tales" and things of that nature; but take it from your brother James, such things are very real and factual, for I have seen many of them since I came into this center of Shamballa as an initiate. As to methods, and I am an old practitioner in diagnoses, you will need to do something more about analytical methods and diagnoses than you do today. It will resolve into more than the taking of pulse, blood pressure, reflexes, and case histories. The patient must be taken back as far as he can remember, even by hypnosis. Perhaps psychiatrists will need to depend either upon themselves or upon some type of clairvoyance; or they may need to train people who are specifically endowed with the clairvoyant training, people who will be able to peer back for at least several hundreds of years into the patient's life to find where he incurred his particular difficulty.

Now, I know this may sound very outrageous to some of you who have gone through medical college and yet never heard of such a thing as an obsession; but I have seen numerous examples, not only over here, but on the earth as well. Those of you reading these lines may be in doubt. Therefore, you may ask the channel who brought the words from me into your present day, for he himself has had numerous experiences with such types of obsessions, working as he does with the doctors and the initiates from Shamballa. Together they are quite able, in most cases, to remove some very stubborn obsessions. I am not quite sure of this point at the present moment but my very dear friend Dr. Pearce thinks if he can get the material together a little later he also may give a transmission. We are not attempting to conduct you in any center in Aureleus; but to explain further, we have come directly into your home through another dimension and, as you know, my entrance was marked by the strong odor of my Corona-Corona. When the time comes that Dr. Pearce gets himself together sufficiently to make his transmission, he will give you more information about practical diagnoses and methods of eliminating obsessive entities which may be possessing a patient's mentality.

As you see, I have spoken little or nothing on the philosophical subjects. I believe that they have been quite adequately covered by many of my predecessors; although the whole subject is quite vast and assumes staggering proportions. We have tried to present philosophy as a factual and integrated working part of the measures in which we here in Shamballa project our guidance into the destinies of mankind on the earth plane as far as we possibly can. However, the principle must remain intact: that man is essentially his own boss: as you have said his own judge, his own jury, and his own executioner; in some cases, that is very true.

Much misery, suffering, degradation, crime, and numerous other fallacies of human nature so openly exhibited in the material dimensions could be avoided by the simple application of human kindness and the elements of understanding and brotherly love. (The channel was concerned regarding the amount of recording tape remaining when Ruth answered that there was plenty.) My dear Ruth, do not expect me to fill up the tape! I am very interested in that electronic contraption which you have. It is a very wonderful thing, although we have different types of electronic equipment in the various centers over here with which, no doubt, you will become acquainted in some future day, in some evolution, especially if you join us here in our 'little' family circle at some future time.

May I say also that R. W. Emerson is standing very close by, and although he had planned to come in tonight, at the last moment he was like the swimmer who touched the water with his toe but found it too cold, so he will come in a little later. His discussions too are primarily ones which link man with his innermost nature. I liked the discussion last night which was given by our very worthy official here in Aureleus. The concept of the personal Christ is a very wonderful and a very worthy one which should be thoroughly thought over by every individual. The day is fast approaching when there will be a reformation in religion on your earth plane. Such old religions and concepts as have dominated and coerced the peoples for many hundreds of years must pass into the oblivion of history. The various scientific and mechanical means of communication on your earth at this time have made the average individual somewhat of a college graduate, as far as his own personal outlook on this world is concerned. Even a high school boy knows much more than some of the graduates of the older universities. Thus if you were in my position and could compare the difference in time, even from my day into your present time, you would be amazed at the progress man has made, not only in the scientific fields, but also in all the kindred sciences of medicine and psychiatry.

The aeronautical industry at the present time is very wonderful in itself; however, I do get quite a 'boot' from the various controversies over the flying saucers. Don't expect me to get into this subject, because it has been very thoroughly covered; and there would be some antagonism in certain circles if I were to explain my own personal views on this matter. However, there are some people on the earth who are playing with matches, when it comes to flying saucers, space travel, and so on. It would be much better if they solved their own problems in their own immediate dimension before getting out into space and encountering conditions with which they are totally unfamiliar. However, the nature of man is such that he has always cast his eyes into the skies and wondered and wondered and wondered. And yet paradoxically enough, he has limited his observations to the concept that he believes only his earth plane contains vegetation and air for the support of life. He will be very much surprised when he finds that there are human beings existing in other dimensions who do not need vegetation or air, and yet thrive very well on what just seems to come from nowhere; things he does not see or hear, just as his TV set picks up the pictures on the top of the hill. These pictures are not seen until they are properly integrated by the circuits which are involved in the mechanism of the set which projects the image on the fluorescent screen.

Thus it will be when man evolves into dimensions which free him from the inhibitive thought processes which he has incurred in the reactionary philosophies taught him from the time of his birth. Universally and without exception, the science, philosophy, or whatever the subjects which have stimulated the mental processes of man in the past several hundred years, but especially during your own time and place, have one common fault: man is trying to evaluate the whole cosmic and celestial system of creation, re-creation, regeneration and incarnation, and all subjects contained in the progression of mankind; yes, he is even trying to confine it to and start it all from his *own little earth plane.* Now that is most illogical; man will never gain access to the innermost secrets of the universe about him until he frees himself from the concepts which hold him in the dimension of the physical flesh and material world. He must first evolve into his mind that mass, whether in the form of his body and its constituting elements or in the mass and energy of his home, the various structures of his city or even the earth itself, is only the result of activity and of idea and of form from other dimensions. Mass could not possibly exist in this earth dimension until it had first been conceived and brought into existence in some other dimension in a higher form. I might say that man's little earth is the last place in which ideas manifest as mass and form. There are very few worlds which are lower than the earth, and material worlds is what I mean essentially. The most important thing to remember in whatever direction one assumes in transcending in personal evolution or reincarnation, the one prime factor which should always be uppermost in the mind is that one shall never come to the time or place when anything which cannot be conceived, cannot actually be or exist in the consciousness. That is the Infinite Nature of God. One will never get to the borderline of God's Infinite Nature. Just remember that, my dear brothers and sisters. Until you hear from us further, may the Peace of God be with you.

— William James.

CHAPTER 65

Good evening; Charles Pearce speaking. It is only fitting that I should follow my very dear friend James; and I believe he mentioned the fact that I would give some discourse along certain lines of psychiatry, which at your present time is not too popular an influence. I was very pleasantly amused by your reaction to his usual entrance with what he calls a Corona-Corona. In case such activities may be misunderstood or some of the puritanical minds may raise their eyebrows and say, "So, they smoke cigars in Shamballa," I will say that his cigar is merely his means of identification or his trademark. No, James does not smoke cigars; he gave up that practice many many years before he became an initiate here in Aureleus. However, as he was constantly seen with a cigar on the earth, he has used this as a means to identify himself in the minds of the few individuals with whom he has mentally or spiritually communed. A large number of the habits, ideas and expressions on the earth were given up or, shall I say, gladly dispensed with and replaced by much more intelligent ideas and practices, which enabled us to take the necessary steps into this beautiful and magnificent planet of Hermes.

I believe William promised you that I would give you a discourse along the lines of obsession or exorcism and other facets of psychiatry which in your present day are quite unknown or at least, shall we say, ignored. In order that at a future time such knowledge and wisdom may be brought into general and more advantageous usage, I shall present some of the things about which we are constantly learning in these centers.

First, do not confuse the word exorcism or the casting out of evil spirits and devils, as concepts which you know in the earth plane expressions as manifestations of these practices which have been witnessed in the savage and more primitive states of mankind upon the earth. There are in medicine, psychiatry and other fields of sciences many levels of practice and understanding. The idea, of course, behind such practices is that they recognize spiritual influences of ulterior or vampirish motives or that such spirits are so misplaced as to impinge in the consciousness of unsuspecting individuals in their daily earth life.

In order to better understand these things, we must go into a more scientific concept of mass or matter and energy. Some of these concepts were explained to you in previous transmissions and were strongly emphasized in the transcript from Venus. However, knowing as I do the failure of the human mind in its ability to retain certain truths or concepts which are alien in nature, knowing also that such concepts must be placed repeatedly within the consciousness to remain, I shall go further into the scientific concepts so that you can better understand, not only the principles which underlie the incurrence of various neurotic or inhibited subconscious differences, but also that you may understand a great deal more in the factual interpretations of your various evolutions through what is called dimensional time and space.

I shall fire my opening gun and direct it especially

at my fellow scientists on the earth by saying with absolute conviction, there is no such thing as a solid. I shall repeat, *there is no such thing as a solid.* The solidity of mass in your world about you appears to be such only because it is a comparative concept which you have learned to accept, not only through your present earth life from infancy, but also in the associations which were impounded into your psychic body in your past lives and incarnations. I know that is a strong statement to make; but I shall prove it in two different ways. Any scientist, nay, even high school students, will agree that such elements as you know of in your chemistry or physics are atomic compositions. You also understand atoms to be certain structures which are composed of supposedly positively and negatively charged particles revolving around a nucleus. For a moment I shall skip to the other proof.

If you had been developed in your mind to such a state of consciousness as was the man Jesus that your concept of energy was conceived from the higher dimensions, you too could walk on water or through supposedly solid masses. Your knowledge of such structures would give you power to alter the frequencies and you would pass through them just as light passes through glass. Although glass in itself is composed of two opaque substances yet the very oppositions in their nature render their vibrating frequencies such that they are so cancelled that they effect the light frequencies in a certain part of the spectrum only in a very negligible degree. Therefore you see the seven basic light colors passing through glass in more or less the same intensity; consequently glass is transparent.

We shall further enlarge our concept of the atom. You have compounded the hypothesis that an atom,

as I have said, contains positively or negatively charged particles. This is a rather crude summation. I shall
try to present to you the factual interpretation of what
an atom really looks like.

Take some small spherical object, for convenience, the size of a basketball, which we would say was
a blown-up atom. We could see it as a mass of tiny
wave-forms that would be lines of force, if you can
call them such. They are *not* atoms or *solid* particles;
they are *revolving around* the spherical compound.
These wave-forms, revolving in a dimension and
vibrating in a frequency which is beyond the com-
prehension of the earth physicist, will, of course,
naturally have certain parallaxes. The main parallax,
which is a conjunction, will be the central nucleus of
the atom. Scattered throughout the spherical portions
of this globe-like mass of energy will be other wave-
forms meeting and crossing each other in a series or
number of different parallaxes. Wherever these different wave-forms cross and re-cross each other their
crossing will be marked by a vortex. This vortex will
be a compound of thousands or perhaps hundreds of
thousands of different types of vibrations which will
thus be regenerated in the harmonic structures of
the original wave forms which are rotating in their
proper orbits. I have not propounded this theory or
concept by myself, but have been assisted by many
notables here, not only from Aureleus, but from the
central corresponding section of Parhelion.

About ninety years before the time of Jesus, a
man by the name of Lucretius, in a poetic or open
prose form, compounded some very definite theories
about atomic structures. It seems to me that in 2000
years, man should have advanced just a little farther
in his concept of the atom. Just as Copernicus placed
the earth and the sun in its proper position in the

galaxy of the universe, so by now your physicist, with all the scientific paraphernalia and apparatus and the brains of your generation, should have enlarged your prospectus so you should know an atom as it truly is.

I shall also make another statement; as I have said, there is *no* solid substance; and since we have now resolved such forms into masses of vibrating energy, we begin to see that here again, just as you have begun to find in your physics book, such form of mass and energy must be properly related to each other with a certain order of laws which are known as the laws of harmonic frequencies. If we strike a string on an instrument, it will regenerate, not only its fundamental frequency, but many harmonic structures. If a second vibrating chord is placed nearby and the two are struck simultaneously, they will generate third harmonic structures. This is a basic and rudimentary example from which we can formulate a more scientific and elaborate process, which will evolve up into the countless number of dimensions in the vastness of space.

When we have let the idea of frequency relationship saturate our minds sufficiently we shall then be able to conceive all things in our own world, the universe and in the solar systems about us as they are in perfect law, order and harmony with each other according to the laws of these vibrating structures. It makes no difference whether they are the largest suns or the tiniest atoms which compose these suns; or atoms which compose the worlds; or the elements which compose the human body; or even the wave-forms which compose any individual's psychic structures. They are all governed completely and absolutely by this same immutable law of harmonic relationship; there are *no* exceptions, there are *no* differences except in the manner in which such laws are expressed in a different dimension. Naturally you can assume that such orders of atomic structures exist in their atomic weight on your earth (and they number from one to a hundred). It is needless to say that in confining your knowledge to the one hundred elements you have confined your knowledge into a very small enclosure. Throughout the celestial and terrestrial universes are not one hundred, but literally hundreds of thousands of such types of atomic structures, revolving in different dimensions and rates and frequencies, which would be beyond the concept of your finite mind.

Since we have established something of the concept of vibration, we shall go further along the line and discover how it is that human beings can be enmeshed in various other spurious vibrations which are not of their own making. There are a number of types of obsessions, one of which may be classed as the category which belong to the obsessions known as the thought-form bodies. They may be of the person's own generation, for he can induce them into himself by the constant repetitious thinking of and dwelling upon an idea. If a person is a hypochondriac and believes himself fancifully to be ill in some of the physical structures or portions of his body, he may, in his fearful state of consciousness, generate such vortexes of wave forms in his psychic body that they will again regenerate into his physical body and actually demonstrate that very physical weakness.

Referring again to our knowledge of frequency relationship, such a thought-form body may also be incurred or drawn into the psychic or subconscious of any individual through some channel whereby he has let his thoughts become attuned to the consciousness or the vibrational frequency of another thought-form consciousness; just as was explained in a previous transmission in the conception of cancer in the young woman who incurred the thought-form body from her mother.

We can further enlarge this concept by saying that every person is something of a small radio station in that he is both a sending and a receiving set. Through the normal processes of his life, he is constantly radiating his own fundamental frequency as well as receiving the other frequency into his subconscious or psychic structures which is in some harmonic relationship with his own fundamental frequency structure. Every individual has a different fundamental vibrating frequency. No two are alike, but through the law of harmonic relationship, a person can incur or send out such frequency as may be in the second, third, fourth, or even in the one hundredth vibrating category or harmonic structure from his own fundamental frequency. This is a type of obsession which we have classified as the inductive thought-form obsession; and it does not relate to obsessions which come through the actual obsessive or the possessive influence or infiltration of some entity from some of the lower astral planes of expression.

We shall next get into the second concept of obsession. This is the kind which is incurred, as I have previously mentioned, by the actual contact or the infiltration or the absorption of some entity into the frequency structures of the psychic body of the unsuspecting body or host. Under normal circumstances, a person born on the earth, through the protective devices and forces which are set up about him in his own inception into the world could, (and many people do) go through long periods of time in these earth plane dimensions without the occurrence of some parasitic obsession either from the thought-form category or from the more personal entity type. If however, at some time or other in his life, a person thinks negatively and becomes inhibited to a certain degree in a thought-pattern of life, he may generate such a frequency transposition or he may transmit such vibrations into the lower astral orders or realms. These will be received by others who are tuned to that particular frequency or who may in some way vibrate in a harmonious respect in the harmonic structures.

To better grasp the idea of what I mean by astral orders, we shall say that anyone on your earth plane in his right mind and consciousness, has full expectancy of leaving the physical flesh and of going over into some spiritual dimension whereby he will again re-express, in a spiritual way, all that he has lived on the earth plane. In thinking over this concept for a moment, as it was explained previously, you will see that a bricklayer may go right on laying bricks for several hundreds of years. This is the concept of the individual. You would naturally assume that an individual who has thus lived on the earth would not in any way assume a new philosophy or a transposition of life in another dimension of which he knew nothing. He goes right on living the kind of life with which he is familiar and it makes absolutely *no* difference what kind of a person he is.

The whole joker here, however, remains in the fact that the farther away we carry our concepts from the higher dimensional factors in this present life, the farther away we shall find ourselves placed after leaving the flesh, and the less service higher concepts become to us. In other words, if we have not conceived in our minds that there are spiritual worlds and dimensions and new lives and the principles of truth which are impounded by these philosophies then we shall be like the explorer who finds himself in the jungle without his mosquito net and other equipment which would be necessary to prolong his life. If a person is of such low mental order that he is a slave to the material habits of the earth, that he smokes and drinks and vilifies his consciousness with sex and other predispositions of the material world, he will find that such concepts have little or no value in the higher dimensions; therefore, when he leaves his flesh, he will quite likely go right on vilifying himself in one of the lower astral orders. However, he does not remain satisfied with such a life for long; he is quite conscious in the contact with his Superconscious self that something is amiss. Of course he may also have compounded concepts in this vile earth life which are relative to thievery, murder, and prostitution of various kinds. In order to perpetuate these ideas of life into his spiritual life as he now lives it without the flesh, he will seek a means and an outlet to further continue these practices. Consequently, he must find ways and means and expressions of contriving to relive his earth consciousness.

Because various saloons or taverns, houses of gambling, and other orders of earthly life are non-existent in his spiritual dimension, he must, through the rate of vibration which is still within his own consciousness, be attracted and confined to his earth life. In other words, he is earth-bound, and he must find a means to express himself. This he will do by finding a compatible vibration, by seeking out and finding the vibrations being radiated into his consciousness which are of such a compatible nature, that it is possible for him to go directly to the person and enter into the person's consciousness in a moment of weakness. He will thus attach himself into the psychic body or structure of that person and thus influence and dominate him, very often causing him to commit murder or to go about the various wayward paths of life which the entity had lived in his earth life incarnation. Now do not raise your hands and go 'pooh-pooh' because you believe this is not true. It is true and the statistics of your present day and age will prove the correctness of these statements.

Further study of the life of Jesus of Galilee will prove to you that the casting out of evil spirits in a higher spiritual concept is a very real and factual science and believe me it is a science. A practitioner or doctor who casts out these evil obsessions from the psychic body of the individual, must know a great deal beyond the concept of your own present science as it exists in psychiatry on the earth today. He must possess a knowledge of physics and electronics on which I have somewhat elaborated. The theory of the concept of vibration of atomic structures to the relationship of the individual in the different planes of frequency, are likewise reproduced in what is called the astral worlds or dimensions. Such psychiatry also involves clairvoyance, or the envisioning of the lifetimes of any person previously lived in some terrestrial plane, whereby he could incur such obsessive entities or thought-pattern structures. A psychiatrist must also know something of the friends or relatives of his patient who could induce, through their own thought practices, possessive thought-form bodies which would impinge the consciousness of each individual.

A common ordinary practice of such hypnotic or hypochondriac absorption of thought form obsession is manifest in your earth today, as manifested in your smoking of cigarettes. Even anyone who is strongly inclined not to smoke may become ill, even weeks after the first attempt; yet the person persists because of the auto-suggestive practices of friends. This is a thought-form possession or obsession which has crept into the subconscious psychic structure of the individual's psychic body. It is also aided and abetted by the psychosomatic habits of nursing and thumb sucking, which was incurred in his infancy, by which the security of the individual was very largely and very strongly built into his first way of life.

I might elaborate somewhat on the concept of the absorbed obsession as manifest in the present day life of your earth. For instance, in the automobile industry every individual tries to outdo himself by getting a newer and a later model of car each year. The mere thought of seeing someone driving up and down the street with a better automobile is in itself an auto-suggestive obsession. Although beyond his financial means, a man must rush over to the nearest dealer and try to outdo his neighbor. Even the ordinary foods which are consumed in the average American home are much different from those eaten in the other countries of the world, but it does not mean in any sense of the word that the difference in dishes means a difference in the composition of the elements; those foods are just as tasteful as your own corned beef and cabbage or your pie a la mode, although they are quite unknown to the eskimo or the savage in the jungle. This thought is along the general line of concept as was strongly emphasized in the opening sections of the book under the subtitle of Venus. Concept is the all and the absolute of every individual as in the statement that in God's world there is nothing, absolutely nothing, which cannot be conceived, lived, absorbed and remanifested by each individual.

In God's great Infinite Mind there is no such thing

as sin or evil; it is purely the product of concept. Evil is the product of living in an age and time in which material values must be compounded and infractions placed against each other so that the relative values may be weighed now, just as any lesson should be given in truth.

In speaking for the higher minds which helped me compound the words which I have been somewhat instrumental in conveying to you, these truths are not necessarily truths of my own making. They are Universal truths which have been known to exist since the beginning of the concept of man in the Mind of the Infinite God, for these are His concepts. To repeat somewhat, so that the lesson may be learned to its fullest advantage: first, there is no solid; everything is energy. A substance appears solid only as a concept in your mind in its relationship to the other forms of energy which are about you. As was stated before, this is the concept of evolution which has been brought up with you through your various reincarnations through what is called the physical or terrestrial planets. Everything is of a vibratory nature.

Vibrations are caused by wave forms of different intensities or frequencies. These wave-forms in themselves are so shaped and constituted or structured that they have a definite intelligence which they repeat unto the end of time. They cannot be destroyed, but can be regenerated into other harmonic structures which are compatible to their own original frequency. The law of harmonic relationship is the law in which all energy in any dimension expresses itself in relation to any of the hundreds of millions of different concepts which you may envision in your own mind. The same principles in electronic engineering enable the transmitter to transmit the picture and the sound in a TV set in a simultaneous program. It is

547

the same principle of vibratory relationship which is carried on and up into the higher dimensions, by which means you will live in the future; for as Plato so strongly expressed in his philosophical concepts, you must put the utmost understanding, weigh to the very smallest fraction of your capacity, these truths which have been given to you. If you do not learn them on your terrestrial planets, you will be so confounded and confused in the spiritual planets that you will have to reincarnate back into a terrestrial planet, wherein you can again give yourself a chance to relearn these fundamental truths. The whole program, the curriculum of your program, depends on the proper learning and the assimilation of these concepts.

Before terminating my little discussion, I should like to enlarge somewhat on the idea of the concept of what is called the astral world. As was previously stated, there is nothing which you can conceive in your mind, or that you will ever conceive, that does not actually exist. It is a true fact that the astral world, in a pure spiritual sense, exists only in the mind of the individual; and because astral worlds are conceived from the material form of consciousness, as a person has lived in his own state of retarded development, so the individual passes on into the same retarded state of consciousness when he leaves the earth. He may wander in this state of consciousness for a short or a long period of time. He may terminate this state of consciousness in a few years, or it may take him hundreds or even thousands of years; for time has not the same value or the same way of interpretation in the spiritual dimensions as in the physical or material worlds.

Time is related only to the expression of concept or idea, and is not expressed in the revolution of a planet around the sun. There is a difference. In other words, if, in your sleep you dream, in that sleep you can actually live in an hour or even fifteen minutes of time, an entire lifetime. In like manner, in the fourth or the fifth dimension, as they are called by the scientists of the world, time is only a factor which is related to the expression of an idea or a form in an entirely different concept. It merely means that the idea or the form of consciousness is lived in the individual to its fullest expression and has nothing to do with a calendar. The idea which I am trying to instill in your minds at this moment is a concept of cyclic or cyclical transmission. We do not regulate the idea of the transference of energy into any conceived or preconceived dimension which confines itself with the rotation of a planet. Such rotation is in itself a cycle and one which has been set up in the present Gregorian calendar of the world.

In the spiritual dimensions, your earth planet is now no longer in your consciousness. What then will you use to take the place of time? You will immediately, if you have been so wise as to study what cyclical motion is, supplant this conception with a celestial form of time, meaning that the transmission of any energy, thought, or form must be in a cycle. Now it is no longer confined to the idea of time; instead, it is the completion of the cycle. Whether a large cycle or a small one makes no difference because no denominator tells you whether it has taken ten years or 100,000 years. Instead you know that you have completed the cycle. You are no longer time-conscious. You are aware only that you have assimilated the idea, that you have completed the idea, that you have completed the work or whatever particular thing the cycle required of you.

In your life on the earth, you get up in the morning at a certain time, you shave, you bathe, or you do other necessary things, such as eating breakfast, hurrying to the office, or to any other line of work at which you are earning your living. Or, if you are retired, you seek the solace of the rocker on the front porch. In whatever cycle of life you find yourself, it is divided into successions of regular hours, minutes and seconds; and so you have learned to regulate your life by the passing of such time. Now if the five physical senses were suddenly taken away from you, so that you could neither see, hear, smell, taste, nor feel, then what would you do? You would need to supplant the time consciousness, the regular cyclical habit form pattern of the earth, with something of an entirely different nature. You would then have only your spiritual consciousness or your sixth sense to rely upon. Then you would need to institute an entirely different way of life. This is about what will happen to you when you lose that little mortal temple of flesh. You will suddenly be deprived of your five physical senses, because they relate you to your physical world. In your new world you will no longer be able to move about in the same dimension of time and space that you now occupy on earth. You will be compelled to rehabilitate your consciousness completely into an entirely different way of thinking. You will be forced to erase certain concepts and replace them with others. This future step will be much easier if you start doing it now in your earth plane and prepare yourself just a little for the things to come, like putting a raincoat in your suitcase or an umbrella under your arm when you go out for a walk on a cloudy day.

These things are inevitable; they happen to everyone, for there are no exceptions. However, the step is not so difficult as it seems. First, remember that you came here from a spiritual world in which all of these values in which you lived and in which you expressed yourself in such an oriented fashion, placed you in a much more perfect state of consciousness than the one in which you now are. When you were born into this world, you merely separated yourself from this spiritual consciousness, because of the dimensional relationship, to such factors of separation as are incurred in this vibrational frequency, between the terrestrial planes and the celestial or spiritual planes. This was perfectly conceived in the Infinite Mind of God, for purposes which have previously been mentioned, for your own personal evolution to develop your degree of Infinity; because, until such degree of Infinity as perfect and absolute concepts are developed in your own mind and consciousness, you do not become an Initiate, an Adept, a Master, a Lord, or a Logi.

In reading these lines, you will begin to understand how absolutely fallacious the idea that merely to think the belief of some individual expression of Mastership, as it existed on your earth, is all that is necessary for your evolution into these higher spheres of dimensional relationship. It is only wishful thinking; it is primarily an escape mechanism, which is born and bred and generated out of the numerous frustrations and inhibitions which are incurred in your daily life. Only in the presence and in the consciousness of your Superconscious Mind, or your soul, which is actually the life cycle of the individual, are conceived and constituted and conformed the necessary wave forms and vortexes which are of the more Infinite Nature of God.

It is in these compounded wave-form structures that the Supreme Intelligence of the individual manifests himself in his relationship to the higher dimensions. It is this Superconscious Mind that is his actual Guardian Angel in the lower terrestrial dimensions. It is that which is the closest to him and that constantly, as a safety valve on a steam engine, keeps him in a proper coordinated working order. It also makes it possible for other spiritual forces to coordinate themselves with his personal expression. This is all part of the protective mechanism which is circumscribed around each individual in his terrestrial evolution. Without this protection he could not live very long, as he would be completely overwhelmed by the great masses of negative energies which are swirling about him. When I say overwhelmed, I do not mean destroyed; I mean that in the placement of the consciousness of the individual, the earth recedes from around him; he is no longer on the earth. In a pure abstract form, he is merely in the placement of his mind consciousness, as it relates to such dimensional fractions as are conceived in his mind, whether it is the terrestrial consciousness or the celestial consciousness.

What is more easily understood and assimilated mentally here is that the product of the consciousness around you is immaterial, only in the sense that it serves the utilitarian purpose of regulating you to dimensional factors of relationship. In other words, you could exist in a thousand different terrestrial worlds which were of the same similar atomic structure as your own. You could be any one of the thousands or millions of people swirling about you. This whole concept was somewhat explained in the Essays of Emerson, when he portrayed the universal spiritual structure of man as each individual similar to and like all other individuals. To see one person was to see them all; for the same ideas of thought consciousness and other expressions of material or spiritual expressions in any one individual might be expected to be seen in another. The universality of man in his relationship to God was very beautifully expressed in these Essays by Emerson. Consequently, in properly understanding the spiritual nature of man, one sees that his various reincarnations are but links in the chain of circumstances in his progression through the terrestrial planes, which in themselves serve only the useful function of placing the finite structures in his mind in a manner which will promulgate the spiritual concepts, all of which are equally necessary and very relevant to the higher spheres of his spiritual knowledge and wisdom.

Now, my dear friends, I could go on for many hours into these more abstract concepts; but I see that the mental and physical energies of the channel are somewhat ebbing. I do sincerely hope that you have properly understood and can evaluate these concepts, for they will be very valuable to you in your future evolution. A question has just arisen in regard to some of the relative factors which enter into the removal of obsessions and in regard to what happens to the obsessions after they are removed. Circumstances are such that the results from such liberations depend largely upon how the obsessions are removed. As to the obsessing entity, if he is a very forceful and dominating or extremely cruel or perverted character, a great deal more Light is needed to shine upon him to bring him from his prison than if he were a less obsessive person, or one who was merely wandering from lack of orientation. Generally speaking that in the case of the freeing of an obsession from the psychic body of any individual, usually the obsessions in the majority of cases, liberate themselves. We assume that, like some mother who attached herself to the daughter for lack of spiritual knowledge, if she is not a perverted person or is not a wicked person with murderous intents in her mind, then she will, upon the liberation, feel the full impact of the Light or the freeing force; and this will be the way in which the lock on her own prison will be forced open and the doorway will swing wide, permitting her to enter into her true spiritual consciousness.

The average obsession requires very little assistance to be liberated from the obsessive traits of character which he may have incurred in his earth-life. Being firmly attached to a terrestrial or an earth-life consciousness means only that he has amassed a superior preponderance of idea or thought-form consciousness in his psychic body. Usually the Superconsciousness, in its proper linkage with some healing force or therapy, will immediately explode these thought-form vortexes and thus rectify and neutralize them into harmless energies. The person will then be properly lined up to his own Superconsciousness and he can thus place himself in a more factual relationship to a dimension where he can start his spiritual evolution.

In making an observation of my transcription, I see that I have somewhat neglected the proper therapies which might constitute the liberation of obsessive entities. I pointed out that a psychiatrist should be sufficiently clairvoyant to be able to peer into the past reincarnations of the individual, or to intuitively conceive the origin of various neuroses or psychoses in the individual's subconscious structures of the psychic body.

The term subconscious, incidentally, is a very confusing word. It merely relates to the intuitive faculty of properly orienting the individual's conscious mind with the vortexes which will relate him in a harmonious frequency pattern relationship with previous experiences in his past life. These are properly relegated into the dimension of auto-suggestive memory consciousness. Now, in the realm of the therapeutic formula, as well as in the diagnosis of the patient, there is no absolute panacea, as far as the pharmacopoeia of the earth exists. All the compounds in the drug stores of the world do an obsessed patient absolutely no good whatsoever. The sedative drugs or the shock therapies are, in themselves, very dangerous and usually only destroy rather than free a person from obsessive thought-forms. The more logical therapy would be to properly apply spiritual energies in a dimension which would be more factually related to the actual energies as they are contained in the psychic body of the patient, and thus neutralize them. This can be done through a collaboration of mind energies acting as catalytic agencies with the mind energies of the teachers or doctors in the higher spiritual realms. It is very unfortunate at your time on earth, due to the lack of knowledge and practice in these spiritual realms, that very few highly developed spiritual therapists actually exist.

Too frequently the spiritual healings are more of a happenstance in nature, in a somewhat relative way of speaking. We say that by the extreme extension or propagation of mind energies, these powers are sometimes unconsciously regenerated into a spectrum which will be useful to the spiritual doctors and teachers who are concerned with the patient and an immediate or instantaneous recovery is manifested. This, we will say, happens considerably in the mind science groups, such as that of Christian Science, Unity, and orders of that nature; for they are very conscious of spiritual healing, and so intensify their concentration of mind energies that they unconsciously regenerate these proper frequency spectra.

However, they lack in all cases, as far as I can determine, a more practical and a scientific application of the laws of vibration as they exist in the higher dimensions of expression.

In conclusion, my friends, let us say that the future psychiatrist must not only concern himself with the immediate present life, in the nomenclature of the studies of psychiatry, as they are instituted in your world of today; but he must thoroughly indoctrinate himself with the more technical aspects of nature and energy and mass. He must learn to be very highly developed in his concept of the higher laws of mathematics and physics; he must learn clairvoyance and go beyond the commonly known and accepted present-day borders of science, in physics and its allied sciences. The psychiatrist of the future will indeed be a much different man from that which he is at your present time. However, I am giving all due credit to the practitioner in that science, for it has made rapid advances, especially in the past ten or fifteen years, as is true in the case of all sciences. The soul must properly progress so that your present-day psychiatrist will evolve with a much greater and more enlarged concept, which will eventually include the highest dimensionally evolved concepts possible for the physical objective mind to conceive.

I shall await your pleasure and wish you the greatest abundance of God's most beneficent blessings.

— Pearce

CHAPTER 66

Greetings, dear ones; I see that at the present moment you are sitting in the great central temple of Pericles here in the Athenian center of Aureleus. This great temple was more commonly known as the Parthenon in Greek history, and is still known to the people of the present day.

So that you may not feel that you are in a rut or that you have arrived at some stalemate, I might say your visit here this morning was timed to be in conjunction with a conclave or gathering of some of the former residents of the earth, such personages as Plato, Socrates, Pythagoras, Archimedes, Lucretius, and many others of the Greek and Roman philosophers of that age. There are several hundred of these very lustrous and illumined minds who have gathered here in this great temple for one of their periodic conclaves for the purpose of further unifying such philosophies as may be pertinent to their expression in the earth plane dimensions. Now the discourse at this time is given as the combined reflected expressions of many of these personages whom I have mentioned; and as your humble moderator, I shall for the present remain anonymous.

In the previous discussion by Charles Pearce, considerable attention was given to the laws of harmonic frequency vibration and relationship concepts; and because these points may confound or confuse any students who may read these lines in the future, our purpose here this morning is to dispel any doubt or confusion which may arise in the mind of the truth seeker. May I say to each one of you that you already contain latent within you, the knowledge and wisdom which was given to you in any previous texts which you may have read; and your arrival point in your future evolutions into various dimensions will be determined by the actual integrated awakening of the knowledge and wisdom which is contained potentially within your own creation.

Do you assume for one moment that God would be so unintelligent that He would create something of His own nature and fail to compound it with the elements of His own nature? The very virtues and essence of His own wisdom are also contained in every individual and in every one who resides in any spiritual or terrestrial dimension. If we philosophers or scientists here in these centers of Shamballa did not know of the ultimate destinies and purposes of man in his reincarnations and evolutions, we would be gravely concerned with his welfare. However, it is so that in the knowledge of these things, we can patiently await the time of man's arrival and induction into a higher dimension of consciousness.

In the earth about you, you see many people who seem to have adopted a very worldly-wise way of living. They have become so sophisticated that they adopt an egocentric concept. They may gather about in the taverns or places of public conception and indulge themselves in the various platitudes of self-expression as to the merits and virtues of the kinds of foods or beverages by which they are surrounded, and indulge themselves in their various ways and modes of life. They may also guffaw very loudly at some lewd or obscene reference to sexual intimacies and things of that nature; and so they have thus considered themselves very wise and worldly. There are others too who have entered into the halls and institutions of learning and while they may not reflect in their own ways in a personal attitude, they too may know the ultimate destinies of man even though they may not be worldly-wise. Yet they have inflicted in the realm and dimensions of science, such mechanical monsters into your world that they have confounded and confused your way of life and made it into some sort of a mad rat race for survival. There are others too, who open the doors of their churches and temples, and, as priests or ministers, point their fingers and cry loudly, "This is the way to salvation," and yet they themselves do not know to any degree or certainty where they will be on the morrow.

The wisdom and virtues of God's Infinite Mind are not contained in any secluded cloistered spot in your terrestrial dimension; neither are they contained in such worldly philosophies as are expressed in the science and arts as they are practiced; nor will they be found only in the every day or the more mundane walks of life. Rather, they will be a combination. The ultimate wisdom is contained in all of the more esoterical virtues as they function properly in their proper relationship in the dimension in which they are conceived. Have you not looked about you into the creation of all things in your world and conceived the Divine and Intelligent plan for conception? You may see a small goldfish swimming in a bowl of water in the living room of some home; and have you not pondered a moment the obvious fact that the water, in flowing over the gill structure of this small creature, enables him to live in a dimension which would very quickly strangle you; that he absorbs the oxygen into his body just as your lungs absorb oxygen from the air; that his body has been streamlined so that the convolutions of his fins enable him to proceed in an unobstructed fashion through this element of aqueous nature. Yes, even the blades of grass at your feet contain a sermon of wisdom in the art of alchemy, which is not duplicated in the highest laboratory of science on your earth plane. In the processes of photosynthesis, the plant is doing something which none of your scientists has the least inkling of what is transpiring. In the ultimate conclusion of all of the growing, living, creeping, crawling things about you, you will find the answer to creation and to the most perplexing problems of your own nature.

Thus it is we see that all these things within themselves contain the elements of logic, wisdom and reasoning. Does not the newly hatched duck immediately proceed to the pond and embark with his feet to paddle about the surface; and yet he is untaught and unlearned in this newly found art. Do not also many of the other creatures of the dimension around you immediately begin to function in their own dimension and in their own realm, without having been previously taught or instructed? From where does this wisdom come? What is the motivating purpose behind the wisdom and logic of a creature such as a dog which will plunge into an icy stream to save his mistress from certain death at the risk of his own life? Does not the love which motivated the action of that dog supersede and make him logical beyond the realms and dimensions of the immediate dangers to which he has subjected himself? Yes, dear ones, even the act of raising your arm and wiggling your smallest finger involves chemical and electronic processes which would take at least hours of discussion to fully explain to you. Yet all of these things are automatic and without thought or reference to the processes which are involved.

In the empirical philosophical concepts of John Locke, he believed that man was born into the world with the surface of his mind completely polished and untarnished by any thought consciousness. While this may be true in the basic elemental concept of the consciousness of the objective mind, yet the empirical philosophies did not extend into the precepts of the Divine consciousness and into the creative plan behind the construction of the Divine Being which is man. The conscious or objective mind is *not* the man. The conscious or objective mind is merely the *result*. It is the conglomerate association of the innumerable ideas and associations which you have formed in the various plateaus of living expressions about you in your daily life. Your mind may be likened somewhat, as it has been termed, to a telephone switchboard; the conscious thought or action is the result of and motivated by the immediate association of one or a hundred or so past associations. However, this deals primarily with the reactionary processes of life as they have been involved in your immediate sphere of creation. Your whole science of psychosomatic medicine and psychology depends upon this precept of the empirical doctrines, as they were expressed by the earlier exponents of these philosophies. Therefore, by the same token, these same philosophies and sciences of psychiatry are somewhat in error in your world today, because they do not contain the necessary spiritual elements of concepts which enable the psychiatrist to function more properly as a healing agent in the correction of the malformed aberrations of the individual.

We must first conceive, as was pointed out to you, that you are a creature of Divine creation; that you truly are a small segment or a fraction of the Divine

God-Force or Intelligence, as you have termed the Creative Force of all things; and that in the manifestation of the creation of this Divine self, it in turn remanifests itself into countless and innumerable dimensions; therefore it will thus take unto itself the necessary vehicle of expression in whichever dimension it finds itself functioning; and in turn it will create the human body; and in the process of creation, as you express it from day to day, you have no conscious knowledge, nor can you control the creative processes which constantly recreate your own earth body. Consequently you live in many bodies which are actually created for you during a lifetime. This too is a product of that Divine conscious Mind or your true God-self, or your Superconsciousness. This is the Christ in you. This is the part which was not crucified on the cross at Galilee, for it was only the Jesus man who died by the violent act of man. It was the Christ Consciousness of the individual man which resurrected the body in the following days and survived for a number of days and months after the reconstruction.

May I point out to you that you yourself will do this same act in many ways and in different dimensions, through your countless evolutions and reincarnations into the future. You may not be nailed to the cross, as was Jesus; but the body which you find yourself now occupying will pass from you just as surely as did the body of Jesus pass from him. It will likewise pass from the consciousness of the many individuals who are living about you in your day and age, just as they have always passed and will continue to pass. Therefore, be not concerned, dear ones, at the present moment if you do not understand the fundamental laws of harmonics or frequency relationship, or if you cannot conceive the true nature of atomic structures. These wisdoms are contained in the structures and elements of the Divine Superconsciousness of each individual, and link him with the most Divine emanating wisdom from the Central Vortex. By the same token, as you so evolve, you will arrive in the natural sequence and order of these evolutions into the precepts of the Divine Consciousness. It will be just as when you were born into your present evolution and state of growth in your terrestrial planet which you now occupy, in which the processes of eating, sleeping, walking, drinking, and the various acts of conductivity in your daily life were naturally arrived at and in harmonic conclusion. In the same manner, your future evolutions into these spiritual dimensions will be naturally and conclusively arrived at in their proper sequence and order.

The essential ingredients which are so necessary for the attainment of these different dimensional factors of personal concept, do not at the present time reside in your own third dimensional world. You cannot study them at any of your universities or academies, nor can you learn them in any of the buildings which are dedicated to arts and sciences, as they are now expressed in the world. They are, however, contained in your Superconsciousness; as Jesus said, "The Kingdom of Heaven is *within*". The principles necessary for your evolvement into these conscious concepts of the higher dimensions, are the precepts which involve absolute faith. You must grasp the concept that you are absolutely unlimited; that God too is also absolutely unlimited in his expression; and that to be thus progressive, you must be God-like in your movements and in your progression through the different dimensions.

Although God has conceived and contrived the world about you as a place which might be called one of sin and error, yet it is through these various processes that you begin to evolve a natural conclusion or a sequence in your own philosophical progression. As Kung Fu says, "Evil is conceived only in the eyes of him who beholds evil;" consequently you have contrived about you tremendous pressures of guilt complexes which reside purely in the realm of the fanciful imagination of the individual. I need not tell you that if you become critical of another person's sinful or erroneous ways, you will conceive his ways in your own mind; you too become an active participant; and you are motivating and becoming an unwitting victim of the same sins and errors, in your own life. The very object of your life experience and the most reasonable thing to do in your own life is to eliminate the word sin from your mind, as well as the ability to conceive sin in your own mind. As you go about your daily life, you must see that each individual about you is manifesting some of the God-like qualities of his nature. Look first for the virtues which link him to the more constructive and logical processes of life. Do not look for his faults and his shortcomings, for if you conceive the faults and shortcomings of another, you are automatically tuning yourself into the faults and shortcomings of your own nature and the most dominant traits of your own personality.

Another concept to remember is the fact that the wisdom and logic and power of God's Infinite Mind is always progressive and constructive in nature. It is never at any time selfish or personalized within the individual concept. In other words, we must go about us using the wisdom or knowledge which we have imbued into our own consciousness for the constructive and the beneficial welfare of our fellow beings. We must know that if at any time we begin to use the God-like virtues of our own nature for our own selfish benefit, we shall immediately cease to realize the value of these benefits. For the value of these benefits is not contained in any personal expression, but only in the universal perception that man is individually and collectively a universal brotherhood and is functioning as a part of the Divine expression of God.

I might add at this moment that these universal precepts of consciousness were contained in the doctrines of expression of the Avatars who have existed on the earth at different times. Jesus, Zoroaster, Buddha, Krishna, Mohammed, and many others wrote and expressed in their various philosophies these same concepts of the Divine origin and functioning of man in his different dimensions; and so, my beloved brothers and sisters, be not confused in the innumerable and sometimes difficult conclusions in the vastness of the philosophies of the many ages which have transpired in the histories of the earth. Although your libraries in the universities and in the cities about you contain many thousands of books on philosophy, as has been explained to you in these different transmissions, yet it is very obvious that an individual could reincarnate to the earth many lifetimes, reading in each lifetime many of these books and still not arrive at any conclusion within his own nature. Instead, each incarnation might find him only more confused with all this knowledge for which he was not properly oriented.

We must always conclude that the assimilation of knowledge and wisdom must take place and transpire within its proper dimension and with the proper placement of the individual; for one cannot acquire knowledge or wisdom of a concept in a dimension in which he is not functioning at that particular time. It would be against the principle of the creation of man's nature to attempt to learn concepts of wisdom which did not pertain to the God-self in their own proper evolution and in their own proper order. That is why so many people are completely confounded by trying to assimilate the more abstract concepts of frequency relationship and vibration. For example, to conceive that there are *no* solid structures about man on the earth plane, one may think by butting his head against a wall, that the wall is solid, but it is only solid by comparison with his head.

Actually there are many atomic structures in other worlds and in other dimensions which are tremendously more solid than a wall or a man's head; and yet that head could very easily pass through these structures without being momentarily obstructed in any way. The difference is that these other structures would be in a dimension which would not be at all compatible to any direct reversions of atomic structures, as they are contrived and conceived in the elements which constructed man's physical body. In other words, I am saying that man's physical body, and the world about him, is only comparatively solid. Mass is seen merely as the conglomerate form of energy held in some temporary state or form or substance in the element of time. In other dimensions where time assumes a different relationship with such energy or mass, substance will express itself in a different way; and thus mass does not assume the characteristics of mass, as man has associated it on the earth plane. Instead, it assumes some other form which cannot be limited to man's present concepts or assumptions that it will be mass or that it will be energy in any other particular dimension.

As I have said, and shall repeat, the concepts of truth as they are expressed and contained in the higher dimensions would so go beyond the limits of the threshold of earth man's finite consciousness, that these would completely confound him and mean absolutely nothing to him. We could not, in our own understanding and in our own concepts, express what we see in the world about us and in the world above us. This we could not do, because man simply would not understand these philosophies or these ideas and forms of life as we see them. We can only interpret them to him in the language and in the concepts with which he is familiar.

We have continually stressed and emphasized the crystalline structures of these dimensions. This is as close as we can come to describing to man the pulsating radiant beauty of the masses of energy which have been accumulated or formed into the functional orders of buildings and in the relation of dimensions, conceived and contrived in higher minds even than ours, for our use and for our purpose. It is in just such various steps or plateaus of consciousness, which stem from the different evolutions or reincarnations in man's personal progress, in which he finds himself in planes wherein reside atomic structures, if we can call them such, which will be compatible to his own concept or to his own position in his individual reincarnation.

He will never at any time find himself in a dimension in which he will be unable to function or in a dimension which is entirely foreign to him. He will always at all times relate himself immediately, either within his own mind or in a factional and realistic way, with such orders of relationship as he has previously conceived in his mind in the last preceding evolution of his consciousness. His more futuristic aspects of life will be contained in the knowledge and wisdom contained in his Superconscious Mind and being. These in turn give him the incentive, somewhat of the intuitive or the constructive spiritual knowledge, which will make him long for the higher expressions, to return to the more pure and the more spiritual concepts of his own nature.

It is this same longing and stressing for this spiritual consciousness which gives man on earth plane his most heroic and his most spiritual expressions in life. It makes him indifferent, to a large extent and in many ways, to the many laws and orders of life about him. These in turn express their own unity, and in their own way, their own creative fellowship with the Immortal and the All Conceiving Mind of God.

So do not attempt to confuse yourself by looking upward, may I say, into the high dimensions which are beyond your present reactionary plane of consciousness. The elements of understanding in these dimensions will have to come through the more intuitive and more highly developed centers of your own personality and from the Superconscious Mind, and concerned more in an intuitive form or fashion. They will have to be visualized as something in the ultimate of your own personal destiny, something which will have to be arrived at and more satisfactorily concluded in your own relationship; and thus you will begin to understand them more thoroughly.

Just as a small infant will eventually learn to stand upon his legs and walk about the room, so you too will learn to function and to arrive at a more conclusive way of life in a higher spiritual dimension which is not so confined and impounded with the factional differences of the time and space and materialistic elements with which you have learned to function and live in your daily life on the earth plane. As Pearce explained to you, everything is vibration or is in some way a wave form, or, if I may use the word rather loosely, an electronic structure as it relates itself in the natural order and conclusion of expression which is called the law of harmonics or frequency relationship; for such structures as wave forms *generate and regenerate* themselves into various different frequency spectrums in properly ordered rates of vibration which are somewhat similar to and can be equated into mathematical formulas. However, for the present we shall not attempt to explain to you these principles, which would be in themselves something of a more advanced understanding in the realms of pure spiritual calculus.

In the days of Pythagoras, when he lived in Greece hundreds of years before the time of Jesus, he somewhat expressed the relationship of vibronic structures and chords and the multiples of tones and overtones, or harmonics, as they were generated and regenerated with the expression of energy, which fluctuated from the plucking of a string or from the sound of a human voice. Into the extension of these earlier vibrotherapy or healing concepts of Pythagoras have been conceived and constituted organized concepts of vibratory construction in the terrestrial plane today.

The radio upon your table contains the basic fundamental frequency wave of the transmitter, which can be said to be functioning at so many kilocycles; however, the music or the voice is further impounded or reflected into the basic wave form structures of this fundamental frequency through the structure of the instrument itself. In the same manner, the healing qualities of the more Divine nature of man are impounded into the various movements or expressions of his own personal life upon the earth through the human voice. For instance, someone who knows something of the principles of healing, and thus the Spiritual Power of his Superconsciousness can work with the conglomerate wave forms of other

Superconscious Minds, as they exist in the more highly developed individuals from these advanced planes, by being reactivating agents sent into the human body of those about him.

Likewise the absolute and complete concept of a man's faith can generate a structure of harmonic chords which will work with the existing spiritual forces in the dimensions in the more spiritual realms; and these in turn become agents whereby certain physical and even mental retardations are, by these therapeutic values, reconstructed, because these wave forms and energies can be properly projected and instituted for therapeutic cures.

There is absolutely nothing happenstance about the functional orders and relationship of frequency vibration, as they exist in the dimensions with which you are more immediately connected. There are no individuals on the earth plane who possess more spiritual qualities than you yourself. The difference is in the concept at which the individual has arrived in his personal progression. If one person has evolved or reincarnated through spiritual dimensions and existences which have enabled that individual to conceive in his conscious or objective mind, the power and the ability of this Superconsciousness, in the absolute abstraction of all values as they are conceived in the Superconscious Mind, this more direct and complete linkage and this understanding and knowledge and working with this Superconscious, will enable the individual more thoroughly to infuse or propagate the therapeutic values of spiritual healing in his daily life.

These powers of healing will not, in a common sense, be felt as bolts of lightning; nor do they manifest themselves as a blue ball of fire, nor other physical phenomena that may be visible to the human eye. An individual may walk about in his daily existence and through the unconscious virtues of the Superconscious Mind, as they are projected through the psychic body structures which link him with his objective mind, he is automatically projecting into all things about him the higher and more innate spiritual values of his own nature. It is thus that he determines his relative greatness or usefulness to his fellow men as they exist about him in his terrestrial dimension. One may thus become priest or minister, humanitarian, nurse or scientist, who gives some beneficial boon to the race of mankind.

So in your daily walk of life and in the hours and moments which are yet before you in your terrestrial dimension, learn more factually, to relate yourself to the Creative Divine processes and to the divine concepts in the commonly accepted and little realized of God's Infinite expressions about you. Look upon the things which are growing, moving, evolving about you and see in them the patterns of life, the evolution, the reincarnation of spiritual values, as they are conceived in the Infinite Mind of God. Try to see that everything has a Divine purpose, a plan as a conceived concept, and that you yourself are existing in your present evolution as the most highly developed and the most complete expression of this God-Force about you in your present dimension which you now occupy. Thus in conceiving these numerous virtues of spiritual values about you, in your future evolution you will have these same necessary qualifications of conception or perception which are so very essential to your spiritual growth.

Do not forget for one moment that as God is Infinite in His nature, so you too can become infinite. You must understand that the infinities of the creative world about you are in their own proper order and in their own proper relationship; for as Jesus said, "Sufficient unto the day is the evil thereof," which, when properly translated, means that you should be sufficient in the expression of each day and of each hour about you, because you have learned some of these factual differences of the creative processes which are involved in the life about you. In other words, what I mean to say is that if you do not learn the comparative values of these spiritual values of these spiritual concepts in the terrestrial planes in which you are now, as has been previously stated, you will reincarnate with your own will and volition back into some terrestrial dimension, in order that you may properly integrate the concepts of mind which are necessary in your evolution.

You cannot hope to attain spiritual maturity in some higher dimension until you have mastered the more elemental and the more fundamental concepts which relate you to the more basic relation of God's nature in the lower plane of creation.

To become a Master merely means that you have mastered wisdom and knowledge in their proper and essential order in your own consciousness, to the point where you can conceive and can work with and manifest these same principles of creation in your own self. Thus you become God-like in your own expression; thus you are a Master.

My beloved brothers and sisters, in your earth life, since you are so attached to the consciousness of personal identity, I shall close by saying that at one time I assumed the identity of one known as Manu on your earth plane. I am here at the conclave in Aureleus at the present time for the best interests of the directional Governments here in the seven centers of Shamballa, although I normally function in my service to mankind in the first section of Parhelion and in some of the higher dimensions which are more properly related to the individualistic concepts or, as you have called them, Lords or Logi. However, there is an integrated pattern or concept which relates us and unifies us in all our efforts. There are no great ones or small ones in these Celestial dimensions, for we function only in direct proportion to the knowledge and wisdom which we have properly acquired through our numerous incarnations and evolutions into the spiritual dimensions. Until such future time as I may serve you, may I remain thus, the humble servant of mankind.

CHAPTER 67

Hello, everyone! Heavenly days! I thought I would never make it. This is R. W. Emerson, or at least I signed my name that way while on the earth, back there a few years ago. There has been a good deal of coming and going since I made the first contact with you about a week ago; and since that time I have heard several discussions and stood around a few times while you were inspecting some of the ancient ruins in this great city of Aureleus. Just joking, of course, when I say 'ancient ruins' for they are really very wonderful and beautiful structures, as you have seen.

Now in regard to philosophy, it may be that we have reached the point at which some of you may be getting just a bit tired of the subject and wish to go into something different; but as some of the material I am using is prepared, and in it are some very necessary steps which must be taken in our progression, we shall proceed somewhat along the lines of a summary of what has previously transpired, so that we may better be able to extract the proper ingredients which were intended to be conveyed into your mentalities.

The prime and motivating conception behind the various interpretations was meant to assist you to think more clearly and to evaluate more wisely your present-day philosophical concepts. As you have been told, there is a great deal of science in everything that

you do; however, there is also a great deal of philosophy, philosophy in poetry, in music, in literature, and
in science itself; in fact in every concept or manifestation of life upon the earth plane.

Since our main discussion or transmission concerns the ancient and modern histories of the world,
particularly that beginning with the Hellenic Age,
about 600 B.C. (At this point Ruth mentioned that
she thought the speaker was present in this dimension, and he immediately received the thought and
answered). I shall reply in answer to that question,
that the lesser of us luminaries here in these cities
do not attempt to conduct you bodily, (I mean spiritually) into the various centers of these cities; rather,
we conduct our discussions more by a telepathic communication.

In returning to philosophy, I hope that by now
you will have looked into some of the history books
of the earth and read the biographies of several of
the great philosophers, musicians, poets and literary
giants who lived on the earth during these various
periods of time. In becoming somewhat familiar with
the translations of these various arts, sciences and
philosophies, your mind will begin to form some very
distinct impressions; namely, that any person who
begins to individualize within his own mind certain
concepts of truth, whatever forms of truth these may
assume in an outward expression, be they prose, poetry or music, these concepts are truths within themselves and are so universally manifested within the
conscious mentality and the Superconscious Minds
of all individuals; and so in themselves they must
relate to each other as individual expressions, either
partially or to a much larger degree.

You may think that there has been a great deal of
borrowing of ideas, or at least a modifying and an

enlarging of them. There may be others who come in at that particular time and scream very loudly at the top of their voices that it is not so or they too are interjecting a slightly different perspective of vision into the general summary and into the idea-form behind the whole philosophical concept.

Such explanations can be seen in the previously mentioned empirical philosophy of John Locke which was conceived chiefly with the material aspects of the mind, or the objective consciousness. The theory was that a child coming into the world presented, as far as the material mind was concerned, a clean and polished surface on which was written, during his lifetime, his numerous experiences, which formed all of the basic concepts of his life. Now this theory was somewhat in contrast with that of other philosophers, George Fox, the Father of the Quaker Movement; John Calvin, the Protestant reformer; Martin Luther, an early protestor, all of whom interjected much more of the spiritual nature into their philosophy along the lines of the more orthodox concepts in the ecclesiastical orders of the various churches which were in a functional order in that day.

Another very apparent fact is that these philosophies contained nothing of the higher spiritual concepts which concern the psychic body or which deal with dimensions of the spiritual plateaus which have been given you in these various transmissions. These omissions can readily be understood inasmuch as the men who lived on the whole continent of Europe had gone through hundreds of years of subjective tyranny in all forms and phases of life, even to the control of a man's thought. We can understand that even the very mildest projection of an individual philosophy would strike like a bolt of lightning through a community or a countryside. Very often the

exponents of these new thought forms were impris-
oned and suffered martyrdom in different ways. So if
some of the higher dimensional concepts were missing from some of these earlier forms of philosophy
during the Reformation era, we shall understand that
strictly repressive factors entered into the structural
forms of these philosophies.

Going back into the Hellenic period, for instance,
we shall find that Socrates and Plato, as well as their
Roman contemporaries, interjected a considerable
amount of spiritual and esoterical values of a very
high order and nature into their philosophic thoughts. If we travel a little farther back into the Herme-
tic period in the Egyptian cultures, we again find a
vast storehouse which pertained to other realms and
dimensions. Likewise in the earlier Brahmanic and
the Vedic concepts, we find in the translations of the
very oldest forms of known literature the answers
to the most perplexing problems which are still confounding the savants of your day and time.

Now there are some other very interesting facets
to the expansion of the various cultures and philosophies in this period of the Reformation that might
be worth mentioning. Although I might say, incidentally, that such interesting concepts are not confined
alone to any person or to any age, yet we could say
that the field of religion or art or science in which
these individuals were most famous was usually not
the field for which they were most fitted. If we study
the biography of Leonardo da Vinci, we find that he
made about 250 or 300 mechanical drawings which
relate to aircraft, dirigibles, and things of that nature
of a very highly advanced science. It was da Vinci who
first conceived the third dimensional perspective, in
which by viewing an object a foot or so away from the
eye, one could see directly behind the object because

of the angle of incidence between the left and right eye. A little later on, a German scientist by the name of Herman von Helmholtz further enlarged upon this stereoscopic concept, to the point where if two pictures of somewhat slightly different perspective were viewed through lenses, the viewer would obtain a third dimensional effect. It was not until the time of Oliver Wendell Holmes, who perfected a working model of a stereoscope, that this instrument made its entrance into the American homes around the turn of the nineteenth century.

This is a good example of what I mean by the progression or evolution of either a scientific or a more simple philosophical truth. You might even say that the concepts of Freud, as they were contained in the ego and the eto, the dominant or the subdominant personalities of the individual, were first explained by Friedrich Nietzche, who embodied the idea that each individual contains the lower or the carnal nature as well as the higher or the spiritual self.

Certain relative spiritual values were also enlarged upon by such men as Spencer and Carlyle, from the Monadic concept of Leibnitz and by other contemporaries of a more remote time. I was fortunate in my journeys to Europe to have met Carlyle, whose beautiful and spiritual nature impressed me greatly; and I was no doubt influenced in some of the works which I wrote, especially the Essays, with his concept of the more idealistic or, shall I say, the universal state of man's consciousness.

In those days of the beginning of my philosophical career, I began to be aware of the universality of mankind in general; for although man as an individual compounds and propounds many elements of individuality, yet one man is the same as another wherever you find him in any particular part of the globe. He exemplifies and personifies or portrays certain universal characteristics, which are found in any race in any part of the world.

Now I was quite proud of my accomplishments in those days; yet as I look back upon them, I know that if I would come back to your earth at this time, there would be a great deal more that I could put into the books or writings of that nature. I would say that even though my writings were fitting to my mentality and expression at the time, yet from where I stand now, they are very elemental in nature.

However, there is something more I would like to say in a general way about the philosophies of the world and about their acceptance by individuals as a whole. Just as I did in my day, you still find people who go around prattling a great deal about this or that philosophy, or pretending to be experts on Shakespearean drama, or they may quote this or that one's personality. Such a person will eventually find himself in a position in which he is unable to express constructive opinions of his own. He will be so entangled and enmeshed in the superiority of his own nature in trying to impress other people, that, as Freud would say, he will be an egocentric. Usually people who are quoting a great deal from the works of others are trying to impress other people with a sense of their importance.

What I am getting at is this: the proper constituents or elements of every philosophy, as it has been explained, are relative to their own time, their own expression, and their own dimension. In your time and your dimension you should extract the elements of philosophies very cautiously, for many of the facts which were of startling importance at the time they were written, are now largely high school talk. The concepts and principles which are evolving around you at the present are of a much higher order and of much more spiritual importance. I would not mean to insult the intelligence of those who previously lived in the earth plane and who expressed themselves in their philosophies.

However, almost without exception, and in a universal accord with my own position, they too, if they could reincarnate in the earth plane, would impound much into their writings which they have learned since losing that mortal coil of flesh. Nevertheless, their truths, as they were written in their life on the earth plane, contained and still contain many elements which are basically very spiritual portions of the concepts which are being explained to some extent in the various occult churches in the world today. In fact, in some cases the truths so propounded are coming direct to you from the centers here in Shamballa.

The whole point I am making is that you should learn to *think, to evaluate* and to form your own philosophy in its own realm and in its own dimension as it concerns you in your own particular lifetime. Bear in mind, just as we do here, that concepts or opinions which you form in your earth life concerning things about you now are only relative to your own position at the present time; and like us, you too will evolve into a dimension in which things look entirely different. You will need to change your ideas and your philosophies considerably in order to get along properly with the conditions which you find about you.

As has been previously mentioned, sufficient unto each day is the evil thereof. I might say sufficient unto each lifetime is the experience thereof and the philosophy contained therein. The most important ingredients which anyone can contain in his philosophy in any generation or in any reincarnation are the concepts which deal with the infinity of nature, of the All-Creative God-Intelligence, of the limitless vistas of so-called space, which a man's soul or individuality contains within himself in making these evolutions into these different dimensions, as he adopts the bodies which are necessary in order to function in that particular dimension. There are many planes and many astral worlds in which one will take on whatever body-forms which best suit the conditions and the nature of the atomic structures and elements in that dimension.

To the earth scientist I would leave just a word concerning the atomic weights and structures of the one hundred odd elements which are contained in your earth at your time: for everyone that you can classify, there are at least a thousand more in a spiritual dimension somewhere around you, which you cannot classify. We here know of basic structures in atomic forms and in transmissions in frequency spectrums which would not only defy the concepts of your earth scientists, but would in some cases completely break up some of the instruments you might try to use to determine the frequency and velocity of the propagations of energy.

I am not a scientist by nature, but I have seen enough evidence around me to know that in the future the approach to true atomic power and to the full realization of magnetic powers which are in the etheric voids which you call space, should be approached gradually and with a great deal of caution. Should man ever tap these vast resources of celestial energy, he could very easily completely blow the planet earth apart and render it into a cloud of dust. The atomic and the thermonuclear explosions, as they have been conducted on earth at different times, have very definite repercussive effects in other dimensions which are more closely associated with the earth planet and are dangerous by virtue of their nature. They may trigger some chain explosion in other atomic structures which compound the crust of the earth and render the little planet earth into something of a burned cinder. This and other portions of transmissions and warnings of the atomic power have been previously given, so I shall not dwell on those points further.

We shall continue with our little discussion here and try to illuminate a few more of the points of some of the previous transmissions. My good friend Galileo some time ago explained some of the concepts of creation as they are contained in the spiritual dimensions. You might close your conclusions in this transmission by conceiving that everything in your earth plane as you see it about you now, regardless of whatever the substance or form or shape, has been previously conceived in some other spiritual dimension in the Divine eye and Mind of the great Intelligent Force which is called God.

Man, in manifesting in the terrestrial planes of consciousness, brings with him when he comes and takes with him when he leaves, the essential ingredients of his entire character and individuality; and contained therein is a psychic memory consciousness of all that he has been, as these dimensions are not concerned in the relative sense of time or space. What is more, he contains not only all the things from where he has been, but also all of the things of where he is going. Therefore, in living in the terrestrial planes and looking about you, you are seeing the ideas, forms and creations of expressions which are the divine components of man's own individual nature. The God-Force or, as it has been explained to you, the personal Christ in each and every individual, conceives and creates in his own prospective dimension whatever things are compatible to the life and the expression of life in that dimension.

There is nothing unrelated or unrealistic in the divine concepts contained in this expression, for they all contain within themselves the necessary and proper ingredients which are conducive to man's life in whatever dimension he finds himself. What this whole concept resolves itself into is that whether God is man or man is God, we cannot separate the two, nor are there any differences contained therein. The Infinite Nature of God must express itself, not only infinitely, but also finitely into every conceivable way and even beyond the ways which are conceivable to your finite mind. Individuality, as it is expressed in mankind, is the individual personification of God, which is manifest in the individual Christ Consciousness. That is the universal principle which I tried to express in some of my writings.

As you have been told, these discourses and transmissions are properly screened and censored for any personal or biased opinions; therefore in the deliverance of these expressions to you, I have come under the direct surveillance of the Higher Minds and Intellects in these various centers; and they have given me the full nod of approval in the material which I have amassed at this moment for delivery at your doorstep.

I am flattered somewhat that the leeway was given me to interject portions of the work which I conducted at my time of reincarnation on the earth. However, this is done purely in the interest of philosophy. Since every man is Divinely inspired and guided by his Superconsciousness or his Christ self, very often in the evolution of time as he lives on earth or on allied terrestrial dimensions, this Christ Consciousness often comes in an intuitive or reactionary way into the consciousness of the individual; and it may inspire him into the most heroic efforts of his life, or it may inspire him to give to posterity illumined sections of truth, which have been inspired from the higher sections and realms of the Celestial dimensions.

Now for the future, there is nothing at which I might point my finger and ask you to read, other than to ask you to search diligently. Read much of the more ancient histories and philosophies of the world, and try to extract from them the principle elements of spiritual truths. But in the general consensus of evaluation and opinions, as you form them, always remember that these are but stepping stones in the evolution of your own personal consciousness into the higher realms and the Celestial Mansions. So until such a time, my dear ones, until we can renew our acquaintance and our further discussions of truths I remain your brother in spirit.

— Emerson.

Note

May I add a P.S.? In looking over my notes, I discovered some omissions which I had hoped to include in our discussion. I neglected rather sadly to mention something which was close to me then and still is, relating to the expression of philosophy in poetry and in music. We cannot neglect the philosophical content of the works of the giants of the musical world: Brahms, Beethoven and Bach. The message of spiritual evolution, the conquering of the carnal self contained in the spiritually interpreted musical philosophies of Wagner's Tristan and Isolde and Parsifal are classics which will endure for many more centuries. The poetry of such poetic geniuses as Goethe, Keats, the Brownings, Shelley, Tennyson, Wordsworth and Longfellow cannot be overlooked. They sounded the golden trumpet which heralded the immortal voice of spiritual consciousness which rang within the mind and the domain of every individual. The immortal classics of Shakespeare, in dealing with the natural sequence of emotional values and of the intense portrayal of lives of individuals in various realms and dimensions of the earth at his time and place, will also endure in the halls of immortality.

The men of medicine and of psychiatry, as they exist in your world today, had their beginnings in the contents of the various exponents of the philosophies of arts and sciences since the beginning of time upon the surface of the earth. In looking into the biography of the French philosopher Descartes, we find there the first discussion of the focusing of the eye, the curvature of the lens, which is the basic foundation for the science of ophthalmology in your present medical field. To the doctor and to the chemist who take great pride in the antibiotics of penicillin, streptomycin, aureomycin, and other of the germ-killers of your age, need I say that these antibiotics too were included in the pharmacopoeia of the doctors and chemists of many a bygone day. Although the remedies were not known by these names, yet their miraculous and curative powers were included in simple remedies for boils, sores and other lesions of the body. The humble pod of the poppy seed and the mold of the stale bread contained the necessary and vital ingredients which are necessary for your present day products, your penicillin and antibiotic drugs. I need not mention that there are accounts during Queen Elizabeth's time and in the thirteenth, fourteenth, and fifteenth centuries, of people with heart conditions who used an infusion of leaves from the foxglove. Today this extract is called digitalis and is still a valuable curative in heart conditions, just as it was in that day for the same condition.

You may take a great deal of personal pride in the spotless cleanliness of your laboratories, your hospitals, and your operating rooms. You may also take pride in the vast accumulation which is contained in the research of the exploration of the various branches of medical and psychiatric sciences; and yet that too is but a small portion which must be achieved in the future dimensions of man's life upon the various planets of the different solar systems. So wait not upon the present day nor upon the achievements contained therein; but search constantly beyond the limits of the present horizon: for truly over the hill are contained other valleys and other vistas and other worlds to conquer.

As diseases of the past have been conquered and eliminated, so new menaces to the health of mankind shall arise and take their place. In your present day understanding of psychiatry here too you have just begun to learn. The future contains many concepts and truths which are beyond your present concept, just as they are being explained in the pages of this book. But now I fear I have overstayed my time and so, adieu again.

CHAPTER 68

I am a former Englishman by the name of Charles Darwin, who lived on the earth around the 1800's. It is with a good deal of something more than pleasure that I have been enabled to come to you with this discussion. I might say, incidentally, that I have just within the past few days made my ascension into Aureleus. I have been laboring long and mightily in the fields of biological research in some other planetary systems somewhat more spiritual in nature than that of the earth.

It was with a good deal of chagrin that I learned that my philosophies on the earth have caused so much controversy and friction between the ecclesiastical philosophers and those of a scientific nature. In my writings at that period, I left two different books, one, "The Origin of the Species", in which I set forth very definite principles, after some scientific research which made it necessary for me to journey around the earth and to visit various archipelagoes and continents; and thus I set forth these principles of evolution in the specifications of plant and animal life on the earth. I did, as many other philosophers and scientists also have been doing and are still doing. I was not clairvoyant nor did I have the knowledge of looking into the spiritual dimensions around me in order to integrate factually the necessary conclusions of these evolutionary sciences. Therefore, my work was somewhat incomplete in its nature as you will see farther along in our discussion.

Now, I was at that time a very religious and pious man, and with my family knelt in prayer before the morning breakfast to ask the assistance of the Almighty God; therefore it cannot be said that I was without religious foundation. However, I am most anxious to clear up some of the conflicts which have been and still are in existence in the philosophies and religious sciences, as they are contained on the earth today. As you read my books and glean their precepts of the evolution of the species, you will see that the amoeba, the one celled protozoan, through certain environmental or hereditary factors, for example, by artificial selection of his environment, may, in the process of many generations, evolve into a multiple-celled creature, one which possesses more than one cell. As this chain reaction is started he may eventually find himself as one of the higher forms of life in the structures of the various biologies of the earth.

Now, the part which I did not include, nor was it purposely omitted, as I said at that time neither my fellow man nor I had the knowledge to peer into these dimensions, was that each earth life of the species in which he was involved at that particular time was only one of many different lives in which this same creature would find himself in different periods of his evolution in other terrestrial planets, which are scattered about this great universe. The creature, whatever his species, is constructed from the same principles of life as that from which man himself is constructed; and that he must therefore necessarily follow the same plan and path of reincarnation as man himself. The difference is that man is the highest and most exemplary form of life portrayed in the various planetary systems of evolution. Man alone possesses the one outstanding and dominant characteristic: the ultimate virtues of the Almighty God, the All pervading Wisdom, numerously referred to in different ways. This God within man is his Christ or his Christ Consciousness. This is the distinguishing factor between man and the lower orders of animals and plants, as they find themselves in the various stratums or plateaus of the spiritual dimensions.

So we see that the amoeba, in his evolution, is not necessarily confined to this small terrestrial planet earth; for this same amoeba has a spiritual counterpart, since he also was conceived before he became an amoeba on the earth as part of God's Divine conception. God would not let even the smallest amoeba pass from His consciousness by the death of this tiny creature. The amoeba also evolves in some other terrestrial planet in some other part of God's great universe. He may at that time be of some other form or nature; instead of having one cell, he may possess two cells. His digestive system may be somewhat different from the vacuoles of his anatomy of protoplasm, as he expressed it on the earth plane, and so on, and so on, ad infinitum.

Now you can begin to understand more easily how it is that the various other planets, whether of the more material nature as your earth, or whether of the more highly evolved spiritual nature, are being replenished and re-supplied with all of the essential ingredients of environmental factors which are contained in your own earth dimension. We see in these various terrestrial and spiritual planets, many of which you know nothing, numerous great cities, peopled with mankind of different races, and blessed with highly evolved plant and animal life, just as on your own planet earth. In the case of the spiritual planets, the plant and animal life is very highly evolved and takes on a much more beautiful expression not only in appearance but in reproductive mechanism and in the way in which it manifests itself in a general way.

In previous transmissions, Mme. Blavatsky and several others dealt very specifically, I believe, with the conception of the Shamballas onto the planet earth at a period of about a million years ago, and with the influx of the Aryan race, which propagated the seven basic root race structures, as they exist and will exist on the earth in a future day. I might say, incidentally, to those who doubt and would like verification of these truths that they might go to Cashmere or Pakistan, and there in these northern provinces on the western side of Tibet, they will see tall beautifully-formed people with very light textured skins, with blue eyes and blond hair; and their mingling with the darker races from the more southern countries might be very puzzling. It was these pure Aryans who passed through Siberia, as it is now called, and into the Nordic countries of Scandinavia and England, and became known as the Teutons, the Norsemen, and the various other segments of the countries as they exist in your time. I might also point out that the original concepts of Druidism, as they were contained in the Celtic, the Pict, and the Gallic religions, were further evolutions from the original Aryan or the Vedic sciences.

Now this may pose a question in your mind. How did the Aryan people come onto the earth in the beginning; and this, incidentally, involves the greatest of truths which I have been able to contain in my discussion. An understanding of factors of evolution in the transmission of plant and animal life into the higher and more basically conceived forms of life, should eventually have, as a natural sequence, the evolvement into the form of Homo sapiens, or mankind. The science of the earth has jumped at this conclusion quite readily, much to the dismay of the ministers and to other exponents of the more Biblical concepts of Adam and Eve in your ecclesiastical doctrines. The pure concept of God, conceiving man as the Divine Creation, would have, of course, no part in the sequence of evolutionary factors from some of the more primitive types of apes which exist on your earth today. So the scientist as well as the geologist and other researchers have been constantly searching for the Pithecanthropus Erectus, or the missing link of the earth; however, he has yet, fortunately, not succeeded in finding a direct specimen of this so-called missing link. He has found several skulls or bone formations in the incrustations of the earth, which related man to some primitive era, such as the Piltdown man and other such findings.

I might say that at the time of the inception of Shamballa there were such primitive forms of man living on the earth. They had not yet fully evolved into the erect and more mobile types of bodily mechanism, in which the man of today functions with the greatest of ease in his own natural environment. It was also assumed by some researchers that man has existed on your planet for something like five million years; so it is not illogical, or without the bounds of reason, to say that Shamballa started about a million years ago. However, bear in mind that man, as he evolved from the lower stratum of earth life on your planet, has not ever assumed the proportions of the species of mankind known as the Homo sapiens of your time. He did get up to the position of anthropoid apes, the gorillas and chimpanzee, and to other slightly more advanced specimens. But here, because of an evolutionary nature and a Divine plan which was in

593

the original concept of the earth, the natural progress and evolution of these creatures was stopped, and for these various and obvious reasons: to bring the Aryan race into existence and thus propagate upon the earth planet the numerous races and nations as they now exist.

There are some other basic concepts which I would like to explain, which have heretofore been omitted for the purposes of avoiding some confusion in the minds of those who read these books. The philosophies and facts were a simplified version of the spiritual evolution of man into other dimensions, a simple ideology of the formation of the psychic body, which links man to his true spiritual self. Now what has been given is true as far as it goes; but for the obvious reasons which I have mentioned, there is a good deal more to the evolution of man in the spiritual dimensions as far as the bodily structures are contained. The concepts of Theosophy, as explained from the various orders on the earth, by Blavatsky, Leadbeater, and numerous others laboring in these fields, conceived that the soul or the spiritual being of man is composed of different bodies and of different forms, similar to the skins or layers of an onion; and man sheds these various skins or layers as he ascends into the spiritual domains.

This is quite a crude summation, but is something which very factually does exist. The psychic body, contained within the dimension of your physical body and functioning as a connecting link between your physical self and your own true Superconscious, will and does, through the various evolutions, pass from you as it now exists. There is within the structures of this psychic body vortexes or waveforms which too are going through evolution. They are being taken away from or added to in a manner which might be compared to the various skins of the onion. This is readily seen if you will pause for a moment to think of the very wide differences in the frequency spectrums of the different dimensions wherein God's Radiant Energy exists as His Divine concept, in manifesting itself in everything which you find about you. In the same manner in your evolution, you will find similar principles explained in the books which I contrived to write upon the earth during my earth life.

These same evolutionary principles are essentially correct in their own way of transmission, shall I say, in the flight of your soul into the higher dimensions. With the principles of environment and the factors of hereditary aspects at the foundation, you will relate yourself to certain harmonic frequency relationships from time to time. You will thus be able to construct the necessary spiritual or even physical bodies, if I can term them thus, which will enable you to function in a higher dimension, just as you do in your present physical and material dimension. My dear ones, may I say that I am not alone in these concepts. Many others of the newly ordained Initiates with me in these high centers of Shamballa, are, with a great deal of gratitude, permitted to come to you with our texts, which are largely compounded, not from our own philosophies and concepts, but also influenced and helped by the higher minds around us.

I may say that truly I shed my psychic body in my emergence into the center here in Aureleus. The initiation ceremony was similar to one which you witnessed in Coralantheus and in breaking through these flames, the very power of these wonderful and tremendous energies dissolved the various vortexes which were contained in my psychic body, which linked me to the earth planet at my time of living there.

I do not now have the psychic body which I once had when I lived on the earth plane. My body now is composed entirely of energies which are of a much more highly evolved nature, so that I, too, in appearing in my actual or physical form, (using the word physical rather loosely) might appear to you as some sort of a flame or a creature shining with an intense radiation, shining both from within and from without. Even though I am describing myself to you thus factually, I am doing so with a great deal of humble reverence for the great minds and intellects with whom I now associate. It is indeed a great and sacred trust, and quite naturally I shall not at any time renounce the concepts and the privileges which were placed upon me at my emergence here into Aureleus. I only wish that I could add, in the language of the earth man, a suitable description of the wonders which I see about me and of the great and wonderful Lords who at times make their appearance here among us. A description of Serapis was contained in a former transmission in which he appeared to us to be lambent flames. Thus you may gather from my remarks that there is no end, and indeed there is no end to the evolutions into the spiritual dimensions which man has before him, if he will so will himself and so contrive within his mind to use the great and expansive nature of the intelligent and Creative Force called God, which the earth man has at his command.

The visualization of a personal God is quite naturally an illogical conclusion in any philosophy which you may contrive in your minds; for it belongs to the era in which you believed in Santa Claus and various other tales of folk lore. Such a belief contains no semblance of continuity with something so great and wonderful as God, who has conceived the innumerable material and spiritual universes; and all of the forms of life in existence in these countless trillions of planetary systems and universes, which exist within and without the dimensions which are perceptible even to your own physical eye. You have arrived at only one very small portion, even in the most highly evolved concepts as they exist on the earth plane today; for earth concepts are but a very minute fragment of the actual picture of the entire concept as it exists here, even in these centers of Shamballa.

So, dear friends, by all means in the future, try to separate yourself from the finite ideologies contained in the earth plane philosophies which are only relevant to your own time and place as a necessary adjunct to the proper functioning of your present evolution. In the plan and scale of life, you must ever look forward to the Infinite conception of God as He is manifesting Himself to you; and thus you will become part of that God in His infinite number of expressions, which at the present you cannot fathom; but they are the numerous concepts and planes or dimensions at which you shall eventually arrive. So, dear ones, until a future day, may I hope to be of service to you in some future relationship.

— Charles

May I also add my small P.S. I have, in my anxiety, forgotten to include one very important point which I wanted to make in my discussion, one that may still cause you to wonder, without further explanation. You may be concerned in your minds about the origin of the Aryans who populated the plains around the great spiritual city of Shamballa, as it existed in the Gobi Desert of Mongolia, at something over six or eight hundred thousand years ago. These people were a nucleus brought to the planet by the higher minds in a materialized or dematerialized concept of another planet, which is several million years in advance in its nature over that of the earth.

For purposes of identification, since location could mean nothing to you, we shall call this planet Ceres, since it is a name which is linked to the old Roman pantheon of God. Ceres was the mother earth and so their planet will be called Ceres for reference purposes only. These people in their evolution at that period of time had arrived at a point where there was a certain parallax, I shall call it, at which some of the various orders of that planet wished to evolve and to repopulate some other dimension in their sequence of reincarnation. The point I am making, is that they may or may not have known the actual will or volition of their spiritual minds; however, they were transported to the earth and became the nucleus of the colony which grew into the Aryan race.

For the benefit of the astronomer, he need not search with his telescope to try to find Ceres, as it is in a more remote section of the great Celestial universe, which radiates in a pinwheel fashion through the cosmic element called space. The planet itself, about twice as large as the earth, is a very wonderful place; and if you could visit this planet in some future reincarnation, I would advise you to do so. Many people from the earth evolve into this planet and there manifest about a step higher in elevation in the spiritual progressions into which you will evolve at some future time. On this particular planet, the inhabitants do not use vocal cords; they have long since discarded the use of speech. Mental telepathy is used almost solely, and they have a very unique form of writing.

Other expressions of life there would be very curious and would cause a great deal of consternation among the various orders or educational centers on your earth today. But, dear ones, I cannot explain too many of these things, since the book is necessarily confined to your own relative dimension and to the various spiritual orders which are contriving to bring about the expansive program which is necessary in the evolution of the spiritual consciousness of each individual man as he exists in these various planets.

So again it is not goodbye, but until I see you.

— Darwin.

CHAPTER 69

May I come in and chat a while? I am a former Englishman who lived on the earth around the 1600's and was known as Isaac Newton. Almost everyone, even a small school boy, is familiar with the story of Newton, who discovered the law of gravity, by sitting under a tree and having an apple fall on his head. Well, now, there was a little more to it than that. However, that story will suffice to identify me with other works which I left on the earth, relative to some of the more specific interpretations in mathematics and calculus, in the astronomical or astrophysical concept of that day; and, coming as they did during the Reformation, those very black days of human intelligence, they fell like a bombshell.

It was not until the time of Planck and Einstein that my concepts were further modified, and were thus more factually correlated to science and physics in your own dimension and in your own time, which made possible some of the fundamental knowledge of the atomic science in your age. I hope that by now you have been able to conceive that there is some sort of a semblance of continuity, or a preconceived plan and purpose, in what at first seemed to be rather a sporadic condition, like the tides that recede and rise again, into the various times of the earth. There are actual conceived purposes and plans on the part of the higher intelligences in the great Celestial universe.

A short time ago a very worthy brother of mine named Darwin gave a rather intelligent discussion about some of the concepts which relate to the biological evolutions of the various species of plant and animal life on the earth. Since Darwin was born only a hundred years or so later than myself, his theories (along with those of an Austrian monk named Mendel, who postulated very definite concepts in the field of genetics) were also somewhat in the nature of a bombshell, coming as they did into the still darkened regions of the ever-expansive evolutions in man's consciousness.

Darwin was particularly concerned and so emotionally disturbed that he actually wept, when he learned that he was to give a discussion for the books which you are now compiling in your own dimension. Because he was so very vitally concerned in this study during his period of time on earth, he disliked to see that his findings were not enlarged upon further, and that the spiritual concepts involved were not expanded and interwoven into his philosophies; and the possibility that these philosophies might, in future evolutions, retard the progress of man's thinking in the earth plane. The nature of these philosophies is such that, while they may expand in their own time and dimension in one place they may also retard in another time and in another dimension. The important thing to remember here is that the evolution, or the progress of man in his various dimensions, is necessarily progressive and because man is infinite in his spiritual evolution, and basically, so is the nature of all things, he too must maintain the constant flow of infinity into his various progressive cycles.

We might best exemplify the retarding effects of certain philosophies in the field of astronomy or astrophysics, as they are conceived at your time; earth man is still conceiving earth as the only planet in the entire cosmic universe which can be peopled or populated with intelligent forms of life. Such a theory is a direct contradiction to the supposedly actual and factual intelligent processes which a man is supposed to be able to conceive, in the dimensions of his own mind. Any person who can, by means of a telescope, view the heaven, or even objectively observe his own earth around him, and not conceive within his mind that there must be other dimensions, that his own earth must be linked in the regular and progressive cycles of these dimensions, must indeed be a very ignorant person, and one not worthy of carrying the banner of a philosopher or of a scientist or even of a theologian.

The friction between the fields of the ecclesiastics and material scientists is one in which there is a distinct cleavage, and one which has been very productive of friction, inasmuch as neither of these two factions understand the integrated concepts of God's Infinite nature; for it is absolutely impossible to postulate any spiritual philosophy without also integrating the basic fundamental concepts of creation and science into such concepts. Likewise, it is equally impossible for science to exist without the spiritual domain, and the interpolation of the spiritual relationships into other factual dimensions, and in the progression and evolution of mankind in such other dimensions. One taken alone is equally as useless as the other, in the final and general conclusion of the theologies and philosophies of any earth in which man finds himself. Your earth is particularly in a very retarded condition because of the generation of friction between these two elements. There is still a very strong adherence in some scientific circles, particularly among certain scientists, into a very adhesive relationship with the pure material dimension. This is quite true in regard to many of the astronomers of the earth today, since they envision their own planet as the only place on which mankind can or does live.

Referring to Darwin and his theories of the evolution of mankind, here again we shall say that there is a great deal of timing being done in the delivery of these various discourses and transmissions into your dimension. It is quite conceivable that we are very vitally concerned with the earth and its progression; and consequently we do know, factually, what is progressing in all fields of expression in your various and daily earth lives. I do not mean to infer that we peek into the privacy of your bedrooms, or into the very intimate recesses of your material lives. Such things are of no consequence or value to us; but we do follow the progression of your mental and spiritual philosophies, and your conduct toward yourself and your fellow men.

One of the reasons for Darwin's rather hasty emergence in the delivery of the discussion into your dimension, was that it was timed to coincide with the publication of a certain national magazine, which is in great demand in your American country at this time. It is the policy of this magazine, at various times, to include in its text very beautiful portrayals of some segment of archaeology or geology, compounded by the various scientific factions existing in your country today. ('Life', on the very date of Darwin's transmission, had several pages on evolution, November 7, 1955.)

Some time ago this publication issued a vivid text about creation of the earth, and the epic of mankind upon it. I shall sum up my own personal opinions by saying that they were very pretty pictures. I shall refrain from pointing the finger of criticism at the efforts, or at the ones who engendered these drawings or illustrations; for they represent years, or perhaps a lifetime, of effort in their field; therefore, I shall not belittle these people in any sense of the word. It is rather unfortunate that, as a result of these publications, great masses of people will further submerge the more objective reasoning processes in their own minds, by accepting these things at their face value, rather than to use them correctly, as merely a basis from which to form a more abstract concept of their own. Here again the scientist has made one vast and staggering mistake. He has at no time in the expression of his doctrines of philosophy ever included anything outside his own terrestrial domain. Consequently, he has, like a squirrel in a cage, gone around and around with these philosophies, which leave him factually no nearer the end with a conclusive philosophy than he was at the beginning.

For instance: in one of the pictures, a man was picking up a fragment from a volcano as the source of fire. (May I remind you that Prometheus was chained to a large rock, a vulture eating his liver, because he stole fire from Heaven.) I am merely pointing out these different ways in which fire is thought to have been brought into expression on the earth. It is a childish concept to say that man picked up fire at any particular period of his life. He always had these things with him. They were direct and natural adjuncts to his way and expression of life. A fiery bolt from Heaven could have ignited a dead tree in the forest, or the simple striking of a flint, or in numerous other ways could fire have been delivered to mankind. All in all, the magazine gives a rather unfactual and misleading interpretation. Primitive man of such mental stature would be inclined to run away as far as possible from any such volcanic eruption. He would not have been concerned with the more immediate values of fire in his daily life. Man, as portrayed in the picture, would long since have evolved into a dimension of consciousness in which fire had already become a daily part of life. He could not have cooked his food, had he eaten cooked food, nor performed the various other functions which would enable him to maintain even the lowly portrayed section of his life.

One of the issues which caused Darwin the greatest consternation was the episode of the Pithecanthropus Erectus, or the Java Man, found by a Frenchman some years past. From the cranial structures of this supposedly missing link, and the few fragments of fossilized bone lying about it in the strata of earth, the archaeologist compounded and created the hypothesis, that here was the missing link on which he based his entire concept of the creation of man. I can point out to you that in some future day, should some super race of man migrate to this planet, and should they find some Mongoloid skulls buried deep within the crevices of the earth, they might have a very low opinion of those who exist on your earth at this time.

Among the various races of people of your day, you can find skulls and cranial structures which are quite similar to the Java Man; and by burying them very deeply in the earth and fossilizing them through time, you could quite easily base your entire concept of primitive man upon such findings, even though that Mongoloid may have been the child of your next door neighbor. In fact in some future generation and regeneration of your own life, if you do not tear yourself away from such limited ideologies, you might find your own remains and call them the missing link.

Darwin based his concepts as starting with the amoeba in eons past as the beginning of creation, and continuing on down through the countless millenniums, evolving ever onward through the ancient periods of time. Science in your day is somewhat vague in regard to the origin of life on earth, within such simple protoplasmic structures as the amoeba. If you study your biology, you will find that the amoeba is a simple one-celled protozoa, or animal, similar to a very small semi-fluid mass of jelly, that moves in a rather fluid fashion across the surface of the water. In eating, it simply envelopes itself around the object of its food, and so digests it within the immediate confines of its body. However it might be pointed out that here is life, a very definite life. This same amoeba has sufficient intelligence to divide itself and to become two amoebas; consequently, we say that it is conscious of that creative plan within itself. It's also conscious of heat and cold, and must also be conscious of hunger; otherwise it would not move in search of prey.

From what source did this intelligence come? This the scientist of your time cannot explain, simply because he has not connected himself with the actual creative processes of God's Infinite nature in other dimensions. He merely assumes that out of the slime or ooze, lying at the bottom of the steaming bodies of water, which had seemingly regenerated in that early earth, crawled the first protoplasmic mass, which was the beginning of all the hundreds of millions of plant and animal species that exist on your earth today.

Now it is very nice to postulate such theories, for doing so forms a very simple and seemingly conclusive text, by which a person can actually escape the responsibility of objectifying his reasoning into more abstract channels, which will carry him into dimensions which are not reactive to his five physical senses. When he is called upon to use any constructive reasoning, which will link him with the clairvoyant processes within his own superstructures, he is very reluctant to do so. As a scientist, he must always have the slide rule as a yardstick, whereby he can postulate all of his dimensional theories, as they exist within the realm of his own material world. This theory is in direct contradiction to all that he knows scientifically today in his theories of atomic structures, in which there are no such things as solid particles. The electrons themselves, formerly thought to be solid, have now resolved themselves into wave forms, or vortexes of energy, as we have explained to you.

The scientist in his nuclear theories is becoming increasingly aware of these fundamental facts, and is awakening to the consciousness that there is no material mass or substance; instead, that everything resolves itself into various spectra or regenerations of energy into different dimensions. We are loathe to become emotional about the fact that man, at your time, is seemingly in a very retrograde state of expression. When I say that, I mean in a comparative fashion, for if he could have torn himself away from his adhesive relationship to his third dimension man would have been in a much better position materially and spiritually by now.

The realms of science, whether it relates itself to astrophysics or to the more pure material science, is going through a metamorphosis; and daily the scientist is seeing the former preconceived ideas of his fellow man tumbling like tenpins about him. Just as my theories and methods of calculus have been displaced or modified in your day to suit your dimension, so likewise in the next few hundred years, the

607

scientist will, to a great degree, see a reformation in his own science, which will relate him more factually to the Celestial universes.

If you study my personal biography, it will tell you that after I sat for long periods of time in meditation, suddenly I would arise, go to my desk, and write furiously for hours, frequently standing up. Yes, a type of clairvoyance related me, through my Superconsciousness, into the dimensions around me; so that I was actually able to integrate the laws of calculus and physics into the world at that time. I could, at this point, postulate and give theories to the earth which would be much in advance of the time in which you are now living. However, this would defeat the purpose of the natural consequence of your evolution; for these things must be conceived within your time and dimension, otherwise they will lack the personal essence of the touch of your own personal experience, for which they are contrived. The very basic elements of the structure of your whole being will hinge upon the vital and fundamental concept that *you and no one else*, must integrate these concepts within the dimensions of your own psychic structures. Whether you call them the mentality, or whether you call them the psychic body, or the soul, they are merely the relationships or the virtues of the personality of each individual, who thus conceives himself in each dimension in which he lives.

One more point, which I would like to stress very emphatically, relates to the translation of progress in man, as was published in the journal mentioned above. In placing the various fragments of man, as he was supposed to exist in these prehistoric times, the archaeologist has contrived to fabricate from the Latin or Greek languages, captions or titles which were attached to the portrayals of legendary figures.

These are subterfuges which he has devised, either consciously or unconsciously, for the purpose of impressing his fellow man. I myself, just as many other people engaged in such research on earth, could be guilty of such practices. This delusion is a common ecclesiastical practice among the churches, which has always existed and always will, so long as mankind upon the earth likes to be deluded: for in these delusions within himself, man automatically circumvents the laborious process of objective reasoning. It is a way of letting some one else do the thinking for him, accepting these things as they are supposed to exist, steeping himself in the opiate of his own unfactual philosophy of life.

In referring to man's existence on earth today, Darwin pointed out the most outstanding characteristic between the creation of man and animals, was contained in the rather nebulous parable in the Garden of Eden. Even though it is strictly a materialistic concept, yet in the end, and in all time, man is basically and virtually in a spiritual sense, the creation of the Infinite Mind of God. He cannot and will not exist as man in any other dimension, without such preconception from the Mind of God.

As has been explained to you, each man has his own personal Christ Consciousness, or, we might say, he has combined, within the elements of his own innermost nature or soul, all the elements which are of God's own most Infinite nature; and thus God becomes a personal human being within every individual. The Christ Consciousness, however, is not contained in these other dimensions; instead strictly within the dimensions of man's own material life. Man, as it was explained by Charles, must be so integrated with the various other dimensions, on down through the various layers or strata of expression, as will exist in the coming eons of time, wherever man will find himself.

So there is a distinct and dividing difference between man and beast, bird and reptile, or any other plant or animal life, which exists on your terrestrial planet. In the general evolutions of plant and animal species, as they come and go in the planetary structures whether they are of the same or of a different nature than that of your own earth, in integrating themselves in these evolutionary processes, the most esoterical or spiritual virtues are contained in their own individual concepts, whether they are a water lily or whether they are a small dog. These constant evolutions refine the vibrations or the constituents of wave forms, which compose the spiritual elements of the plant or animal, so that in the end, they resolve into the dimensions in which they will become a useful part in the creation of new dimensions of plant and animal life, in other worlds and in other times. They may, in actual sense, become something of a great reservoir of refined celestial energy from which the great Creative Mind of God draws, so that He may create a more spiritual consciousness of our own individual soul.

However, these principles are primarily abstract in nature, and are not acceptable in your finite consciousness. I shall conclude this generalization by saying that, within the infinite concepts of the Intelligent Mind of God, He expresses Infinity; and, as has been told to you, you will never at any time evolve into any dimension wherein you will be able to see the end of God's Infinite nature; and yet you must at all times see that as Infinity is expressed as such, so it must also contain all of the elements of the finite individual. It is in this finite individualism that God contrived man. The so-called Soul or the Spiritual

Consciousness of each individual, is therefore the Divine concept of man, and resides only in the dimension which is called Homo sapiens. Actually and factually therefore there is no missing link. At no time was man ever so contrived in your terrestrial dimension that he was half man and half beast. If you look about you in your civilization today, you will find many individuals who are still expressing such a relationship; and yet there is the distinguishing difference that they too, somewhere in their evolutions, will find the supreme Soul Consciousness of their own individuality.

The basic structure of the body of man has long been a misleading element in the philosophies and in the conjectures which these philosophies might contrive within the individual's mind. Man may see himself as an evolved hairy beast; but here again, referring to dimensional factors of relationship which are beyond your world, this body is only the contrivance of the expression of the individual; so that he can best function and perform the necessary functions in the terrestrial dimensions, in which he is beginning his soul flight or evolution. So do not forget, whether you are a scientist or whether you are a layman, that the texts of these transmissions are contained within the dimensions whereby most individuals in the earth can so absorb them into their own consciousness. You must always remember, as has been explained to you, that the terrestrial dimensions about you are only the projection of idea or form of a much more highly conceived purpose, from a more highly developed mind, even much more highly than your own Soul Consciousness.

It is also essential for each individual, if he is to become an infinite creature, or is to attain the attributes of his Soul Consciousness, which is the composite form of God's own intellect, to combine therein all the elements and virtues, even to the finite relationship in the great cosmic universes, such as are contained in the lowest animal forms of the terrestrial dimensions. Therefore do not jump to illogical conclusions because, in your haste and panic and seemingly illogical sequences, (or portrayals of emotional minds, as they are expressed in the world about you), you will find that man is ultimately seeking his innermost nature; and he shall at some future day find this ultimate spiritual nature for himself.

At one time when I lived on the earth, I was so contained in the personal ego-consciousness, as it is called, or the personal relationship of self to my fellow man, that it was Isaac Newton who signed the various Philosophies or doctrines which were contrived from my mind and flowed from my pen. Here in the great city of Aureleus I find myself not concerned with Isaac; for, just as you are, I am a channel whereby the minds, the intellects, the great Celestial Mind of God Himself, in some small dimension, can flow into the world about you. Thus it is even unto the future, that, as we progress, we shall find that we always become a more factual and integrated part of that great concept. We shall, in the ultimate destiny of our spiritual evolutions, find ourselves absorbed and recontained, and thus lose our ego conscious in some great sea of Mind Force or Celestial Energy, or, as it is called, God.

When I evolved into this dimension, I found the very nature of the most Infinite God Himself is composed, in its entirety, of hundreds of millions and trillions of such finite individual concepts as my own. It is the projection and radiation of these universal concepts, which have been expressed and evolved and contained in these individual minds, as they evolved into this vast sea, which is called God, or the Central Vortex. It is not one finite individual or some super God or some super Being; but it is, as I have said, the conglomerate intelligences of hundreds of millions of uncounted human individuals who have, eons and eons of time ago, lived upon terrestrial dimensions such as your own. It is this universal projection of their innermost natures into the lower terrestrial and astral worlds, in which we ourselves find that God is thus so contained.

God is thus individualized; yes, and even beyond this great supercosmic sea of millions of intelligences, are also other dimensions of expressions so contained, which are even beyond the minds of those who are projecting from the Central Vortex. Now, my dear ones, sufficient unto each day. Therefore labor not for the attainment of knowledge which is beyond your time or place; but so contain yourself that you will utilize the time of the earth as a cycle, whereby you may best further the experiences and progression of the inward consciousness, so that you need not suffer further reincarnations into these lower terrestrial planes. Thus you will become of greater service, for, in expressing service to your fellow man, you become a part of the great integrated plan of the Divine Concept.

Amen.

CHAPTER 70

Good morning; I am Johann Mendel, a person who formerly lived on your earth, about the time of my worthy brother Darwin. I too had something of an influence on the philosophies and sciences of the evolution of animal and plant life, as well as of man himself, in the concepts as they exist on the earth today; consequently, I was chosen to assist you in the next transmission. To those who are becoming impatient for some more glimpses into these astral and Celestial dimensions, may I promise you that we have more, yes, much more in store. There is still a section of Aureleus which you have not yet visited, which concerns somewhat largely your own America, since we have heretofore confined our explorations to such sections as were more relative to the older ages, as they were in the African and Asiatic and European continents. However, more of that later.

In my dimension of expression of the earth, as I walked about in the gardens of the monastery, I observed many curious things, which enabled me to postulate a theory on the processes of regeneration within the various species of plants which I observed, thereby concluding that these things must necessarily be in some form of continuity, to be re-expressed in each succeeding generation. This study became the foundation of what is known as genetics. As Darwin and others told you, at my time there was something of a theory of spontaneous regeneration, teaching that plants and animals just simply sprang into existence. The exponents of this theory were somewhat vague as to what actually happened; and therefore it was necessary for this fallacious concept to pass from the minds of men. Now, in my own expression on the earth, I had the same common fault as did Darwin and many others, who have expressed either a material science and philosophy or a spiritual science and philosophy. The mistake was that our theory did not include the proper portions of wisdom and knowledge which extended the boundaries of concept into the spiritual dimensions, in such cycles of evolutionary progress as are sometimes called reincarnation.

The modern Christian theologians of your day are still very vague as to what Heaven really is, and concern themselves only with the immediate birth in the one dimension and in the one time, with their extension into Heaven made only through the personal contact of the Jesus Christ. Likewise, the archaeologist is guilty of grave misconduct in his science, although his very methodical research has contributed a large and wonderful science to the earth. In discovering the numerous cities of the ages of the past, he has helped to bridge the gaps which are so very apparent in the evolution of the numerous and the different ages of time, or the different empires of such time. Yet it was firmly proclaimed that the findings of a few mere fragments of cranial bone structures, in some strata of the earth, were insufficient or inconclusive evidence on which to base the great and wonderful evolution of man, as he came and went about in his numerous dimensions. In this postulation, the archaeologist is guilty of misleading his fellow man and confining him into a very small and circumscribed circle of thinking.

So it is with the empirical philosophy of John Locke. We must search very diligently indeed into the more ancient Grecian, Egyptian, and Brahmistic concepts, which have existed in the ancient ages, before we find much of the more factual interpretations which carry man into something of a more spiritual evolution of his nature.

Now we have progressed in the various discussions to the point at which some confusion may be arising in your minds as to the meaning of personal Intercessor, or personal Savior, in the spiritual philosophies, and the reasons for a man to seek out and become a creature of the environment in which he may have been previously incarnated. This particular part of the transmission has been prepared by some very notable scientists such as Tesla; therefore, I shall give these words to you much the same as they were prepared by them.

In order that we may better understand the different ways in which man evolves and reincarnates, and thus comprehend the nature of the personal Intercessor, we must become somewhat scientific, as is the case in the higher dimensions. Your own physical laws, which are relative to the transmission of energy in your own dimension, are very pertinent and relevant to the actual transmission of energies in the higher dimensions. The difference is, of course, in the various factors, such as time and space.

Now to make it rather simple, if it can be made simple, we shall point out to you a familiar piece of electronic equipment, the common ordinary radio which sits about in the living rooms of numerous homes in your America today. The same principles which have entered into its construction are basic concepts which must be understood, if one is to relate himself with the harmonic values of his evolution, and so link himself with the different dimensions. It has often been called frequency relationship and other terms, which as yet may not have been made quite clear in your minds. Now, since your radio is quite capable of receiving several hundred stations you may have wondered how that is done.

I need not say that the messages from the stations which are vibrating in the immediate vicinity of your radio are existing in the mechanism of your radio at all times; but some functioning mechanism separates the different stations, so that they appear singly as the concerted sound and voice structures emanate from the loud speakers. The principle used is the same harmonic frequency relationships, or vibration, found in the life of the individual.

We shall begin by saying that the radio contains several small spools of wire, wound about a cylindrical form, with several hundred turns of this small wire contained on each coil. Now, this coil is so wound as to have its own natural inductive or aperiodic rate of frequency, so that if an electric current of an alternating or pulsating nature can be caused to flow within the various turns, and travels through the dimension of the wire contained on the spool, it will generate and regenerate certain frequencies which are its own natural or aperiodic rates of frequency (or vibration). If a piece of iron is placed in the immediate vicinity, or inside the cylinder, this iron will increase the inductance, and thereby change the frequency or the aperiodic rate into something which is considerably lower than its own natural rate. The amount of iron determines the lowered rate of frequency or vibration. If instead a piece of copper or brass is placed therein, this metal will decrease the inductance of the coil to such a point that now its frequency rate is vibrating in frequencies and harmonics, which are far beyond its own natural immediate reach. (This is, in effect the same as adding or subtracting turns of wire from the coil.)

In your earth dimensions, we can liken this illustration somewhat to the various environmental factors with which you are surrounded. If the environmental conditions are negative or inferior to your own productive spiritual philosophies, they can be said to be of the iron or of the ferrous nature. The negative forces change your own natural frequency rate into such lower dimensions of vibration that they are even farther removed from their own natural rate of inductance or aperiodic frequency, which is its true spiritual relationship. If we introduce elements into your environment which are of a spiritual nature, and which are inspirational and which will further inspire and stimulate the better virtues of your nature, as a consequence, the natural aperiodic frequency of your own vibration is so changed that it will bring you in much closer contact with your own spiritual consciousness.

Now it has been mentioned that there is a personal Intercessor. In the Christian philosophies, this is a very dominant factor which is continually expressed. It is in some conflict with the mere fact that the priest or minister may be teaching hell-fire and damnation; but as has been pointed out, why would it be necessary to believe in hell-fire and damnation, if Jesus could at the proper moment, with some call from you, reach out His hand and snatch you from the gates of the fiery Hell? You would say, "I can live my life of sin and lust as I please, spend a few minutes calling loudly for Jesus, and I will then be saved."

You can begin to understand, if you will think for a moment that man as an individual may have several thousands of reincarnations into these physical

618

dimensions; and there are literally millions, even billions of human beings who are existing, not only on your own earth, coming and going, but they are coming and going in numerous other earth planes of a similar nature. And with the coming and the going, there must be, in these sinful natures, a great number of cries for help to the Christ. He must indeed be a very busy individual and must be possessed of numerous hands to reach out and snatch all of these various persons from the creation of their own perdition. No, my friends, such theories are illogical conclusions which are born from escape mechanisms of numerous frustrations, fears, and inhibitions, which have not been properly rectified and dissipated by the true positive impingements by frequency vibrations, which would cancel out these negative and spurious frequencies.

Getting into this question, we might say that a man can be likened to a swimmer who has gone out into the water, has been overpowered by the waves, and finds himself sinking. He will, therefore, call loudly and someone on the shore will throw him a line or a life saver, or some piece of wood, which will enable the swimmer to save himself; or the person may plunge boldly into the icy current and snatch the swimmer from certain death. This is basically the principle of the personal Intercessor. However, it does not, in any sense of the word, guarantee that the swimmer, forgetting the nearness of his previous drowning, shall not again embark into the icy currents and repeat this same experience in his future reincarnations. How can we say then how many times a man would actually be saved by such a personal Intercessor. No, there is a much more logical and, shall I say, scientific way of explaining these concepts.

A person does have a personal Intercessor, but it

is his own personal self, his Superconsciousness, as it has been called. Under the right conditions and with the proper contact, this Superconsciousness can reach out and does save the individual. However, this is in its own proper order and function, and only under certain laws which are determined within the frequency relationships of such individual. We must first visualize that the Superconscious is in very close contact with the higher dimensions, from which stem the most *Radiant emanating Energies* of Intelligence, called God; and since the likeness and the infinity of these radiant energies is contained within the personal Superconsciousness, man must be an exact portion of this Almighty God.

However, man is living in the earth plane dimensions in the lower and coarser frequency spectrums; he cannot possibly hope to attune himself and make close contact with his Superconsciousness unless, through many lifetimes, he has become conscious of this Superconsciousness, and can, therefore, as you would say of your radio, tune himself into the higher dimensions, wherein this Superconsciousness resides.

The average human being who is living about in the earth plane at your present moment has no knowledge of such highly evolved principles of frequency rate vibration; neither is he conscious of his Superconscious Self, as he should properly be. Instead he is more concerned with the lustful desires of the material world which is about him. It is only proper that he must have the relationship of other dimensions from whence come his personal guides, who can, and do, help in the more intuitive moments of his life, to properly guide him or to try to prevent him from committing some great sin against himself.

This has very often been called the 'Still Small

Voice.' These are the prompting intuitive voices which compose the spiritual guidance, as well as what we might say is the harmonic frequency which comes directly from the Superconsciousness itself. In moments of extreme emotional stress, we can say that a person is somewhat extended beyond his consciousness, beyond the limits of his own dimension, so that the factors of time and space, or frequency relationship, are somewhat altered in their general functional order as they have normally existed. Under such conditions of psychic stress, a person can tune into the higher dimensions or realms, wherein are contained the elements of his Superconscious Self. Thus he will, in these moments, be capable of becoming for a few moments a superman; or he may exhibit such an unusual display of supernormal intelligence that it will be something of a miraculous nature.

Now let us go back somewhat in our discussion, and determine more factually how a man arrives into the material dimension, similar in nature to the one in which you find yourself. We shall call it the material dimension. We shall suppose for a moment that this individual is walking about and seeking ingress into your dimension. He is similar to a hungry beast who is prowling about the forest, seeking food, and is not necessarily concerned with which animals may come across his path on which he can pounce and devour. So it is with the uninitiated entity wandering about the astral world. He is seeking out a means of getting back into the world with which he is familiar. In this manner each person is radiating his own fundamental frequency into these various astral dimensions.

He may also be likened somewhat to a searchlight shining with the different colors, according to the rates of vibration which the person from the physical planes is radiating. Therefore, this astral person, who is seeking ingress into the world, wanders about until he finds a light or a vibration which is harmonious or conducive to his own nature, and in the strongest respects with which he is most familiar. He will, therefore, linger about this vibration until the moment of conception, when he will thus be enabled, in his blunderings, to enter into the womb and into the ovum which is being conceived unto the child.

The child, after coming into the world, will thus not only have the predispositions of the parents, in regard to the numerous facets of the physical body, such as brown or black hair, and blue or brown eyes; but here again the entire personality, as far as the spiritual nature of the child is concerned, will continually manifest itself much as the individual who so incarnated into the body of the child at the moment of conception. He may thus actually become the murderer or the militant leader, or he may become the politician or be in any other particular field with which he was familiar in a previous incarnation.

This will explain to you somewhat, if you will think a bit, why some people know nothing of a spiritual nature. Instead, they surround themselves with a vast amount of wealth; they ride in beautiful automobiles; their homes are majestic with many rooms; and they have done nothing, you might say, which was of a nature that would warrant what might appear to be very munificent blessings. You will begin to see that these individuals have spent many lifetimes in such endeavors, and they are merely reliving these reincarnations. They have actually set up these dimensions of wealth within their minds with such intensity that they are only reliving and bringing into existence these preconceived dimensions of previous existences. And so it is with the others who may be alcoholics or perverts or thieves. They also may just be reliving to some extent these previous reincarnations.

Now you are beginning to understand what we meant when we said that we have omitted some of the spiritual concepts which are necessary in order for man to understand himself properly, in our general synthesis of mankind in reincarnating into terrestrial dimensions. I need not further extend my views to explain that a person, incarnating into your dimensions, can also manifest and will likewise become, if he is a highly developed spiritual man, something of the nature of a Buddha or a Christ or a Jesus; and he will lead many thousands or many millions of people into a newer and a more highly developed spiritual concept. He may also be a doctor and thus bring into the world new treatments or new theories or even new discoveries in the realm of medicine, which will be of benefit in the numerous plagues that have beset mankind.

The principles of genetics, as they were impounded into the basic concepts which were somewhat apparent to me in my studies of plants in the gardens in the monastery, were the same principles understood by Luther Burbank, who will give you a transmission in the future. With his knowledge he was enabled to propagate species of fruits and plants, into the dimension of your world, of a nature very different from those originally intended by the chromosomatic structures of their own life cells, as they were contained in the seed or in the basic psychic structures of the plant itself. Plants, like humans and animals, likewise have psychic bodies. These psychic bodies, just as in the case of the man, relate the plant or the animal to his own dimension in the same factional order, as has been pointed out. The main difference between man and plant and animal is that mankind possesses the Christ Self or Christ Consciousness, which is of the much more highly ordered concept of God Himself, in that it comes more directly in contact with the emanating source of the Intelligence of God. This is the difference.

A person, in his various reincarnations or evolutions in the numerous dimensions, is now getting into the more personal relationship of the Intercessor. You may wonder how this personal Christ Consciousness can reach out through the dimensions and help a person to save himself, for such is the case. If a person, wandering in the astral dimensions, becomes cognizant of the fact that his surroundings are unrelated to his own true disposition, and that somewhere in some dimensions above him there are great and wonderful worlds, he may set about to pray and to cry out so loudly that the vibration of his voice, in its spiritual nature, is of sufficient intensity to reach through and to harmonize itself with the dimensions and planes above. The people in the Shamballas or in other astral dimensions, who are the life guards, will go into these low astral orders, in a sense of the word, and help rescue this individual, as they have done in countless cases.

Since the individual lacks the strength and the efficiency to navigate in the higher dimensions, due to his lack of knowledge, he will thus have to be carried, more or less as we would carry an injured man on a stretcher, and will be placed in some suitable environment which is most conducive to the rebuilding, the recharging, and the replenishing of the more spiritual elements into his psychic structures, in order that they may more properly relate him to his Higher Self. This process has been very largely explained to you in the various transmissions from

Venus.

So in all cases, the problem of the personal Savior, the Intercessor or the Christ, as he has been called, resolves itself purely into the concept of the individual; and the one who finds himself in a low order of the astral worlds must necessarily put into effect the proper orders of relationship frequencies, which will enable the beings from the higher dimensions to function and to assist the individual into a higher dimensional relationship. Therefore, in concluding my transmission and remarks, here again you have been given a portion of the truths, which we here in Unarius learn in somewhat more of an expanded dimension.

I might point out to you that it is most necessary and vitally essential to your own spiritual growth, that you conceive the elements of these truths within your minds before you pass from the dimension of the physical expression. If these concepts are properly learned and placed within your mind, even though you do not understand the more advanced scientific principles, you must remember that within your own consciousness somewhere, there is a storehouse wherein these things are placed, a storehouse which shall become the supply room of the future, wherein you will find that, when you evolve into some spiritual dimension from the physical flesh, you may not within your own consciousness be so concerned with yourself at that moment, for, as a result, you will realize that you have passed beyond the material dimensions, and thus you will not find yourself in some strange environment with which you are entirely unfamiliar.

These are individual factors which are entirely different with every individual; for no two people ever evolve into these spiritual dimensions in exactly the same condition. Just as each contains his individual personality traits, so likewise the composite forms of the intelligence, as it is expressed by the individual, will relate him into the future concepts of his evolutions. However, this storehouse, in which one has placed much which was not understood in the earth plane, can now be reopened, if one will conceive this to be possible. There will be found the treasured truths which have been explained to you. These truths could not exist in the storehouse unless they were of such nature that they could exist in these higher dimensions.

The old hypothesis or the irrelevant factors of spiritual concepts which relate to blood, hell-fire, and damnation, are entirely unfactual and unrealistic, and will not exist in your storehouse; but the other factors, which relate to the dimension of frequency relationships, shall properly place themselves in this storehouse of the psychic conscious, so that each one will be enabled to find the proper equipment which will help him to function in the dimension in which he finds himself. He will be enabled to use it the moment he needs it for his own personal intercession. It will give him the strength and the necessary frequency relationship, so that his prayers or cries for help can extend into the higher dimensions; and his personal forces and Superconsciousness will come down to help him out of his predicament.

So, my friends, remember always that there is a very definite and scientific explanation for everything that goes on about you. The same principles which are motivating and activating all of the concepts of life about you, and even those pertaining to the appliances which you use in your daily life, are largely the same principles of physics, or of law, order, and harmony, which are expressed in the higher dimensions.

The main difference is that they are dimensional in their relationship, and are altered to harmonize with the fashions of space and time and things, as has been previously mentioned.

This itself is evolution. Until such future time, my dear ones, I shall remain ever anxious and ever willing to serve you.

— Johann.

CHAPTER 71

My dear ones, this is Luther Burbank, and I have been waiting most anxiously to come to you. I have been gone from the earth and the flesh for only some thirty years; but even so, much has happened to me in this time. First, I went to the planet Ceres, as did Darwin; for this seems to be a planet which is quite highly evolved, comparatively speaking, in the plant and animal life which comes from the earth; and indeed we can learn much in the higher elements of spiritual vibration, as they are manifested in these somewhat higher astral dimensions. I was purposely brought from Ceres here to Aureleus, and given some sort of an initiation ceremony, so that I would be able to help deliver these transmissions to you. This is necessary because, as has been explained to you, they are relative to your own dimension, and serve as a much more convenient means of bringing them into existence without tremendous or drastic changes in frequency vibration. Several of these persons have been a spiritual godfather to you, and have been a great deal of help and influence in your life. I too would like, if I may in my future evolutions, to assist in whatever capacity that I may serve.

Now getting into the things of the earth plane; if you study the biography of this man, Luther Burbank, you will find that he left several thousand types of plant life which I shall, for convenience, call hybrids. These plants were evolved and were conceived

628

into the world as products from the evolutionary principles, which were explained by Darwin. In other words, the hereditary factors were transmitted from seed to seed or spore to spore in their environmental and natural state by artificial selection. Like many other exponents of the philosophies and sciences in the world, largely or completely through no fault of our own, but from lack of understanding, I also omitted the spiritual concept which rightly is contained in these philosophies and sciences. Therefore it is our avowed intent and purpose to reconstitute these philosophies and sciences into the earth in the future, through such channels as your own mind, so that they may further benefit and expand man in his evolutionary progress.

If you visit your vegetable and fruit stands or the nurseries about you, you may see many varieties of fruits and plants which are entirely different from the original species from which they were evolved. My own town of Santa Rosa, in Northern California, was a place of rare beauty; and I worked long and diligently to maintain the plant life as it grew about the countryside with which I was associated at that time. The processes of bringing these new hybrid species into the world and conceiving them is worthy of some explanation, for these principles may be somewhat vague in your minds.

I shall begin, for instance, with the plumcot and the nectarine, as you know them. We shall take a small sapling, four or five feet in height, which is an apricot by nature and sprouted from the seed of the apricot; and from a nearby plum tree, which is producing beautiful plums, we shall select certain buds. After pruning down the small apricot sapling and making slits in the bark, we insert these small buds into these slits, about two or three feet above the ground. We shall then seal the bark with bees' wax and bind it firmly with strips of cloth, so that these buds cannot be moved or dry out. They will soon take hold and send tiny rootlings into the cambian layer of the trunk of the tiny sapling; and thus these buds will soon grow into several branches on the trunk of the apricot sapling.

Now this first generation of plumcot will be somewhat confused as to its nature. The branch may want to grow apricots and it may want to grow plums; but among the various different tastes in the fruits which grow on this tree, and with proper pruning and selection, you will eventually develop a fruit which is more to your taste and liking, and one which you have conceived to be the ultimate result of your experiment. Then you take this same seed and plant it in the ground to grow a new sapling, and select buds from the nearby parent tree which are also to your liking; and thus you grow a new fruit. The process is repeated for a number of generations, until you artificially select in the growing of these different generations, a fruit which will finally arrive at the type which is suitable, a pure hybrid variety, one which is neither a plum nor an apricot; and thus you now have a plumcot.

I might point out to you that these processes are necessarily complicated; nor can you let down for one moment after you have evolved a new species. These trees and plants must be constantly watched, for they may revert to their original type; or they may suddenly spring forth with characteristics in an entirely new direction which will be unwanted, and will necessarily mean further work for you to eliminate these characteristics. To further illustrate: two men may select from the same basket two beautiful ripe apples. One man goes carelessly along his way eating the apple, and soon tosses the core into a nearby field. The seed will fall to the ground, and from it will spring a seedling apple that bears the blossoms of the apple tree, yet it may not entirely resemble the original parent tree from which it sprang. It may have many suckers and runners and is inclined to sprout small branches, which tend to sap the strength of the tree. The blossoms may smell like apple blossoms, but the fruit which comes from them is not like the fruit from the parent tree which conceived the seed. It may be very small, bitter, and unpleasant to the taste. So you see that in the nurseries, where plants are propagated, a great deal of care is necessary in the continual regeneration of the necessary virtues in each succeeding generation of trees.

It is the same with humans; there is no difference, except that we are evolved in concepts which relate to the human body and to the expression of the mind. However, humans propagated and brought into the world, likewise need a lot of care, not only from the inside, but from the outside. We say that two parents who are very fine people, religiously inclined and very constructive in nature, may bring into the world children who may be complete renegades. This is similar to the apple tree. Like the apple tree, there must have been a very definite lack of the same principles in the propagation in the expression of these children. They were neither budded with spiritual virtues at an early age, nor were they restrained in their own dimension, like the pruning which is done to these trees to keep them from sending out wild branches in all directions at the expense of bearing fruit.

There is an expression which I heard many times on the earth, "From little acorns mighty oak trees grow." In the countryside of California you will see many thousands of beautiful oak trees; and we shall use these trees as a beginning to postulate a new concept. It is not new, but may seem new to you because you have not formulated these thoughts within your mind. If you will examine these oak trees very closely, you will see that no two are the same; they are all oak trees, but each one has a different number of branches. Their trunks are different in circumference or in the way in which they lean or in the way the branches spread from the trunks. They may all have oak leaves; yet essentially each leaf is different, for *no two are exactly alike.* These differences may be microscopic and infininitesimal, but there are differences, nevertheless. It may also strike you that the oak tree may have lived for many years, yes, several hundreds of years beyond the time when the tiny acorn was completely absorbed and dissolved; and so whence did the natural sequence of growth and evolution of the oak tree transpire?

Trees exhibit intelligence, just as do other plants and animals in their dimension and in their own way. In the Southern States is a specie of plant known as the Venus' fly-trap. It is so constructed with two hinged leaves that it can trap and hold and digest insects. It actually has a certain type of smelly bait in the middle, between these two leaves which are spiked; thus the insect, alighting on this sticky smelly bait, will immediately be enclosed by these leaves and digested by the fluids of the plant. Similarly, in the jungles of the hot countries, are species of trapping plants which can trap and digest small rodents.

On the bottom of the ocean floor are sea animals which grow like beautiful flowering plants. They are very parasitic in nature and devour all tiny forms of life which come within reach of their many waving flagellum or arms. In Australia is a species of animal called the duck-billed platypus, apparently, neither a mammal nor bird. It has the bill and the web toes of a duck, the tail of a beaver, lays eggs like an alligator, lives on a diet of earthworms, and grunts like a hog. Now, if you will examine the natural sequence of evolution in the various structures of plant and animal life, as they exist on the earth, you will sooner or later come into the concept that there is a great deal of intelligence which is combined in the expression in all the plant and animal species. The unbeliever, or the person who is not diagnostic or analytical in his nature, may mutter something about instinct. And so, my friend, what is instinct? Instinct is something which cannot be measured by any known scientific device; neither can it be defined in the nomenclature of the scientist, other than the fact that it is a relative expression of intelligence.

The doctor of your time has an electronic device known as the encephalograph, which is a detector of brain impulses; and while this machine may put the wavy lines of brain impulses on a strip of paper, yet these wavy lines do not convey in any way the meaning of the impulses, or indicate of what they are factually constructed. Therefore, we must relate the dimensional concept of intelligence into its own proper place. Intelligence exists as an indefinable quality of vibration in the dimensional factors which are more immediately related or associated with your own environment. The passion flower will quickly close if touched by the finger; therefore, this plant is intelligent. The poppy knows enough to close at sundown so that it shall not waste the brilliant colors which are necessary in its propagation with the insect life which these colors attract to it. Likewise many species of plants bloom only at night, or they cast off their perfume either during the day or at night; for they know which of the various insects or moths that are necessary to cross-pollinate the blossoms, fly about during the daylight or during the night hours, and are therefore attracted either by their colors or by their perfumes. Is this not intelligence?

You have been told that a tree, such as may exist in your front yard today, before it could be expressed in your dimension and live in your front yard at the present time, *had* to exist in many dimensions before it could arrive on your own earth. This is quite true. We have been told of the *infinite nature* of God, and of His expression into the many realms and dimensions, of which there are an infinite number; consequently, the same tree may express a similar quantity of life intelligence and expression in somewhat the same form.

Like the oak tree growing upon the hillside, it may not typify the same number of branches or the same circumference of trunk; nor may it live in the same time period or the same number of years. Its leaves may be somewhat different. If you could visit Ceres, the planet of advanced plant life, you would know more factually what I mean; for here you could see plant life in a beautiful and expanded nature of relationship that defies description. Yes, and even in the higher dimensions, too, the plant and animal life will reach proportions of expressions which are almost fantastic and unbelievable, and would be so in your own language of the earth.

To those who have confined their thoughts to the dimensional factors of relationship which are immediately about them, I say that I have seen these things and can verify the truth of these statements. I have seen plants growing which seem to be nothing more than stalks, wherein is some kind of very beautiful crystal material and on which are hung the leaves and blossoms, glowing with the colors and facets of millions of jewels. The radiance of some plants is almost too brilliant to look upon; and again at other times, they evolve certain relationships downward into the more terrestrial or material dimensions, which you know as the earth planet nature. Such is the infinite nature and relationship of God, in all of the dimensions as they are expressed and in which they are contained.

If you examine the theories of genetics, as they were first expounded by Mendel and further enlarged upon by some later contemporaries, you will find that the characteristics, or traits of character of an individual, were sometimes carried over into the succeeding generations in the ovum of the female or in the spermatozoon of the male germ cells. It was theorized that the traits of character were carried in the structures known as the chromosomes. The theory was somewhat fanciful in nature, inasmuch as it was supposed that there were certain molecular structures which, in some mysterious way, carried over the traits of character.

To carry this theory further, it is somewhat true in its relationship that there are certain molecular structures which are the material or outward expressions of the more inward nature of the atoms, from which they are composed. As you know by now, atoms are tiny vortexes of energy, which are linked to the different dimensions of relationships, in the psychic body of either the individual or of the animal which is being diagnosed. With this psychic body are carried the factors, or the intelligence traits of character, which are supposed to be carried in the chromosomatic structures. In the succeeding generations and in the infusion of the spiritual consciousness into the individual at the moment of conception, so, likewise, like a photographic plate, are carried the impingements of the wave forms, from the psychic body to the cell structures, as they are formed into the body of the individual; and thus he grows within the womb as the fetus. He may thus evolve at the moment of birth; and, as the oak tree does, he likewise grows into an individual who exhibits the physical traits of character which were contained in the original spermatozoon or the ovum. However, the physical characteristics are only the dimensional factors of his own life about the earth plane.

Let us not neglect for one moment the fact that this same process is carried on into the higher dimensions which are related to his intelligence, or to the way in which he thinks. The higher wave forms, or vortexes within his psychic body, have likewise become a part of this physical body, and are constantly repeating and expanding their own relationship to him in his conscious or subconscious mind. Thus he is continually reacting or enacting scenes of his past reincarnations; or he may be re-enacting to some extent or he may be influenced by the childhood happenings, as is now part of the understanding of psychosomatic medicine.

We here in these centers, (and I am speaking for my more highly developed and advanced brothers and sisters), know the finite limitations of the conscious minds of the readers of these pages, due to the firmly entrenched and preconceived ideas which your earth life contains. We know also that sooner or later these truths, through constant repetition and presentation in different ways and through different individuals, will become as a stream of water and will wash away and purify the channels of your mind, to such an extent that you will be further enabled to visualize the true perspective and dimension of truth, as it is contained in these realms and dimensions with which you are associated.

I do sincerely hope that I have carried my points clearly, in explaining that there are actually no basic differences in the evolution, either in man or animal or plant life, in the immediate dimensions with which you are concerned. These things, as they exist in you and on the earth plane, as it is so frequently called, are merely the ultimate or the end expressions of the more highly evolved and preconceived ideas which have been expressed from the Infinite God.

In your lower order of dimensions, you are beginning to learn and to assimilate certain factual differences or comparative values. You will thus learn, within your minds and in your evolutions, the comparative differences between what has been called good and evil; and you finally come to the basic conclusions that all things are, essentially, merely concepts of the mind; for as the individual conceives things within his own mind, so they shall exist in reality to him.

Think for a moment of the lobster or the crab living in the ocean, which can very quickly replace a claw that has been dislodged through an accident; yet you see many people about you with missing limbs; but they are unable to grow a new leg or a new finger. In spite of the knowledge that you grow a new body every several years yet you do not have the conscious power or will or volition properly to institute the necessary progressive wisdom and intelligence into your body to remove certain spurious conditions, known as disease; nor can you grow new limbs, as does the lobster or crab or even the humble little lizard, scuffling around in the grass, which can grow a new tail if one is lost. We must think about these things; for although we may not evolve into a dimension whereby we can grow new limbs, by the proper assimilation of constructive knowledge, we can further regulate our lives so that such accidents do not need to happen: and our philosophy should evolve so that disease becomes unnecessary.

The condition known as cancer, and many other types and forms of disease which are called incurable, in the pharmacopoeia of your day and time, could very quickly be eliminated and replaced by constructive cells and constructive energies in the body, if you had the proper functional orders which would enable the continuity of the constructive life force, which stems from the Superconsciousness, thoroughly to regulate and to infiltrate into all portions of your daily earth lives. But do not expect to evolve into such a concept in the dimension in which you are now living. That dimension was purposely conceived in the Divine Mind of God, to acquaint you with the more fundamental values of equations, and further to weigh and to propagate the basic concepts and philosophies in your mind, which will be more useful to you in your evolutions.

In the ultimate end, even after you have arrived in the higher dimensions, such as Shamballa, and have cancelled out the many negative energies from the psychic body, these experiences remain with you then as positive experiences, or the energies containing the experience quotient in a positive way. However, this also would be negative in relation to the Superconsciousness, since there must always be the two polarities. You will also gain much wisdom which will be of value in your future expressions in the higher dimensions, which are beyond our description, and so it is my dear ones. Do not forget for a moment that the most valuable elements in your progression are not built within the structures of the subconscious mind, known as frustrations, fears, neuroses, and guilt complexes; instead the most constructive part of you will be the knowledge and wisdom which is propounded and compounded from the various elements of good which have been extracted from the experiences of your many evolutions of earth life. Do not in the future ever lose sight of this factor. And so until then, I am your brother,

— Luther.

CHAPTER 72

A good day to you, brother and sister. I am an individual known as Christian Huygens, who lived in the 1600's, in the proximity of Newton's time. As you have studied in the histories of the period of the Reformation, those were indeed hectic times; the very air seemed to be filled with a new essence, which excited and infused the minds of mankind. If you examine your histories, you will learn that, living in Holland, I tinkered some with physics, mathematics, and things of that nature; and that I invented a double pendulum clock, a kind of pendulum which was rather an innovation to the commonly accepted type, which swung back and forth with each escaping moment. I was also in very violent opposition to part of Newton's theory about light. He maintained a corpuscular theory, that light was a tiny minute submicroscopic particle; whereas I postulated the theory that light traveled in a wave, or in an undulatory fashion, through the atmosphere. As you will soon see, we were only partially right, as is the case with all mankind, who live in such dimensions or places on the earth that they can, in their own concept, evolve only a small part of the truth at any time. They must wait until future evolutions and cycles to enlarge their concepts, so that they can more truly ascertain the nature of the great universes about them.

Now it is believed here that you have all progressed somewhat sufficiently with these words, so that you will have begun to form certain definite and expansive ideas in regard to creation, and the numerous laws and forces which are moving about you in different dimensional forms. However, to keep these conversations on a level which will be understood, not only by the scientist, but by the layman as well, we shall draw allegories or similarities with which you are familiar in your daily life.

The whole idea or plan of the law of vibronic vibration, as has been mentioned in several previous discussions, can be likened to the piano keyboard. With four fingers you can strike four notes, which are all in harmonious relationship to each other. This is called a chord. In terms of the physicist, we might say that this is a frequency spectrum. The seven rays of light which you see as light, is the light frequency spectrum, or is the portion of that frequency spectrum (more correctly) which contains several hundreds of different vibrations which you cannot see. These are also somewhat related to other different spectra above and below.

Now, if we had enough fingers and arms and enough piano keyboards—for as everyone who plays the piano knows, there are many hundreds of chords and combinations of chords which can be struck on the piano keyboard—so, if we likewise had a great number of keyboards and fingers and hands with which to strike, simultaneously, all of the chords at the exact instant, they would all produce a great unified concerted and harmonious chord structure, which we could say was a dimension. In a similar manner, you see these same ideas carried into the numerous facets of your daily life, all related to energy as it is manifesting itself in your dimension.

In my time on the earth, Newton expressed the theory of the solid particles, in contradiction to my belief that there was no such thing as a solid particle, and that everything, even though it appeared thus to man, was nothing more than energy. It was this gradual evolution of the concept which began to confound Einstein in his later days; for he openly admitted that he was confounded. Nor can I say that he was alone in his conflictions of understanding; for this seems to be the dividing line between the concept of the objective mind of the individual on the earth, and that which he assumes in a new position in a spiritual dimension.

In a previous transmission a reference was made which explained that space, or the solar system, was similar to a large number of soap bubbles, each within the other, expanding and contracting through each other simultaneously. Faraday also explained to you that the sun was formed from a vortex, like the steps which lead up to a higher level. These concepts were placed in your mind as levels, whereby you could more properly understand a more complete concept of the abstract of the fourth dimensional hypotheses of these equations. The vortex forming the sun is not just one vortex. As we look at it from somewhere out here in so-called space, we may see it as an infinite number of vortexes, all formed around and around, so that it looks like a huge spherical ball of pulsating Radiant Energy.

Now, getting a little closer to this great seemingly wonderful pulsating energy sphere and examining it more carefully, we find that within it are contained many different expressions of energy. These are called dimensions. It is the law of God that in His Infinite nature, as He expresses Himself down through these different dimensions, He is assuming and reassuming a finite expression, or, as the physicist might say, the positive energy flows to the negative and the negative flows to the positive. So it is with man; he is conceived in the very lowest of the terrestrial expressions as a negative being, so that he will evolve in his ultimate destiny back to the positive source and become unified with his true God nature.

The dividing line here in his evolution is not, as was thought by Darwin in his first crude hypothesis on the earth, that man started as an amoeba and worked his way up through the different strata of life on your earth. The dividing line between man and animal is that dimension of relationship with God, whereby God assumes, in a personal way, a definite relationship with every individual man. This has sometimes been called the Light or the Christ Light or the Christ Consciousness, and is (as was previously strongly emphasized) the confusing and conflicting element in the various Christian dogmas on the earth, as they exist today.

Getting back to our great pulsating ball, or sphere of energy called the sun, as we are looking at it and getting into it—for it will not hurt us—we shall see that these different energies are continuously manifesting themselves from the outside toward the center and into different dimensions, and as each dimension regenerates an opposite, which is the law of polarity, this opposite must, by necessity, be negative in nature and thus it must exist in a lower dimension. If we wind two coils of wire and run a pulsating or alternating current through one wire, it will regenerate itself into the other coil which is placed in close proximity and in a parallel position. Here is exactly the same law of frequency relationship which exists in the great spherical dimension, which we are examining out in space.

Just as Faraday told you, the remanifestation of energy, and the regeneration of it into these lower orders of harmonic structures in different dimensions, is thus propagated in a centripetal fashion, projected toward the center of the whole dimension, so that in the end, it may form a sun like your own. Since this energy also is negative in relationship—just as the energy which formed it—and composing as it does, numerous and an infinite number of dimensions of negative energy, which are only negative in proportion to those energies which created it, so it in turn must express this same universal law. It is by this re-radiating of energy into a different dimension which is below it, that it becomes the sun of your earth.

It was the conflicts of this idea, which Planck tried to postulate in his theory of quantum, that energy was expressed into small packages or into some proportions, as he postulated, in a mathematical equation. Actually it was somewhat in this way, except that Planck did not conceive this energy in its true relationship. It is this same general structure of hypothesis, which we have just examined in this spherical ball, which also relates itself on down through an infinite number of dimensions; and so becomes one of these expressions which is commonly termed atomic structures, in the various masses of earth as they exist today.

In the concept of the atom, as expressed by the physicists of your time, there is still some error and some conflict which he should clear up in his mind. First, the atom in itself contains very little, if any, energy. If the atom were disconnected from its source, or from the dimension which created it, it would instantly cease to exist. We must remember that the atom, in whatever atomic structure it is constructed as an individual atom, is supported by an immediate dimension which is just above its own proper order, or frequency relationship. As far as the atom itself is concerned, it is somewhat like this great mass of energy we have just examined. Although it may not be quite so complex in nature, depending on what particular atom it is, yet it is essentially constructed and functions in exactly the same way. It is an expression of a rather intricate form or pattern of energy, revolving or gyrating into the center nucleus of this atomic structure. As the centers gyrate or rotate about, they are regenerating these negative energies, which are forced toward the center and form the nucleus of the atom.

The parallaxes, or places of conjunction, where the different small vibrating junctions of dimensions are joined by their harmonic frequencies, are, in themselves, points of intense frequency agitation, and are sometimes referred to as electrons. In the atomic sciences, in which atoms are pushed or stretched beyond their true perspective of relationship with their higher dimension, in so triggering them, their springing back into their dimension causes them to collide violently; and in the expression of the sum and total, the harmonic structures which are generated by such concussions, thus expel into the world a certain instantaneous release of the dimensional energy which is contained immediately above them.

It is indeed fortunate that the Divine Creator conceived the fallacy of man's own mind in his interpretation of these things, and placed the barriers of the dimensions, so that he could not blow himself to 'kingdom come' with these experiments in atomic concussions. The instantaneous released energy, as it immediately flows into the atom at the time of collision, is sometimes called neutronic energy, which makes the various objects surrounding the atomic explosion radioactive; for it creates a radioactive cloud of ionized particles of this so-called neutronic energy, in a vastly agitated condition in the molecules of oxygen in the air in the upper layers of the atmosphere. As was mentioned by Faraday, a natural conclusion to atomic power is not in the destruction of the atom, but one which would make the atom itself, and innumerable numbers of its companions, an outlet into your dimension that could properly funnel or channel the great dimension of cosmic energies from the Infinite Mind of God Himself into your world, to be used as a useful substitute for the caloric energies or hydro-energies, which are generated in the various types of power plants on the earth today.

Now you have, I believe, amassed a little better concept of the structures that will somehow help to clear up the differences which may have arisen in your mind, in trying to integrate these concepts about the underlying theories of conception of the individual traits of character in the individual, as these theories were posed in the science of genetics. In the original concept of Mendel, when he lived on the earth, the scientists did not know the more advanced theories of energy transmission, or the supporting structures of dimensions above the atom.

They were not aware of the fact that the chromosomes, which were somewhat interpreted as molecular structures, exist in the protoplasmic elements or the spermatazoon; and that it is in the contents of these molecules that the chromosomes are contained in the elements of the individual's expression. This too, is only partially correct, insofar as it goes, because these same molecular structures, as you will see in your world about you, are likewise composed of the same atoms which are, in turn, within their own expression above them. These dimensions, therefore, through the laws of harmonic relationship, are linked to, and are a part of, the properly constituted elements of the psychic body.

At the moment of conception, the individual who enters into the womb of the mother actually enters into the atomic structures, or is intermingled or woven in with these atomic structures. Thus these atomic structures repropagate themselves into molecules, and the molecules into cells, which become the body of the individual. So you can see very easily how it is that the intelligence of these numerous wave forms of the psychic body are reflected into the physical and the mental states of the individual, as he exists on the earth. This also might pose a question, which is immediately dissolved by referring to this equation.

After the moment of conception, the father could disappear or be killed; yet the growth process would continue in the womb of the mother. It makes absolutely no difference to the infant, who is not concerned with the father at all during his growth in the womb. He takes on the characteristics or the elements of his father in direct proportion to how he has been linked to the psychic body of the father through the laws of harmonic relation, just as he is linked with his own psychic body.

He may take on, or reject, certain elements of influence from the psychic body of his father or his mother, according to the expression of these frequency relationships in their proper order and harmony. Thus it is that the mother, for instance, may give birth to a child who, in a former life, was her father; as a result, the child will relate himself in this life on the earth as a very close companion to the mother; for he will have retained, in a psychic sense, all of the elements which will manifest themselves in this relationship in their future earth expression. I do not mean that he will act as a father toward the mother; but there will be a very close psychic or spiritual relationship, which will defy diagnoses in the elements of understanding as they are known on the earth.

Therefore, in propounding and combining these elements of understanding in your own conception, you must constantly refer to the orders of harmonic structures as they exist in the similarity of the piano keyboard, as has previously been explained to you. As the child grows up with his parents, he may look like his mother or he may look like his father or he may combine the attributes of both, or he may be entirely different from either one. The proper understanding of how he arrived at his own individual expression is not necessarily confined to the old basic concepts, which were expressed in the usual understanding of the science of genetics. They must always be understood from the laws and orders of harmonics, as they exist in the dimensions from which all life on your earth must evolve.

An understanding is therefore very important to the parent, lest anyone should become fearful that a wandering or a lurking entity might enter into the womb at conception. This would be absolutely impossible in all cases, if the mother and father entered into the union with the idea in their minds of conception and its divinity, that they were, in their own way, giving an opportunity for some soul to evolve into this world, to work out something of a pattern of reincarnation or evolution. In the proper understanding of life, and the principles involved in this creation, sex would not thus become an outlet for animal passion, as it is so commonly used among the peoples who have a lesser understanding in the world. Sex would not be so promiscuously exploited in the process of life about you in your world today.

It would assume a more proper and functional relationship to its true procreative purpose, and to its own content of psychological balance, as it is expressed in the individual.

Sex, as it is expressed in your world today, is a symptom of a vast exploitation in the numerous social pressures, which are placed within the minds of every individual in his life upon the earth. There are other symptoms of this disease among your civilization. The teenagers of your time are constantly expressing in themselves psychological revolt against the neurotic conditions, which have been induced in their minds from the subversive elements of these material pressures which exist about them.

Neither the parents nor the youth are necessarily to blame, because they are so confused by these pressures and the resulting insecurities, that they continually revolt against them in the more recognized or organized precepts of your social structures. So the young girls run around in their tight fitting jeans, their loose fitting shirts, and their peculiar hair fashions which naturally shock their grandmothers. Likewise, the boys in exploiting their high speed vehicles, called hot-rods, and their numerous other revolts into the excursions of addiction to drugs—marijuana, for instance, and things of that nature—are also expressing a definite revolt against all of the things which have been compounded into your civilization, which have induced these neurotic frictions in their subconscious minds.

All in all, dear friends, this is merely the expression of frequency or energy in the different dimensions of relationship; and thus you have a proper understanding of what energy is, how it expresses itself, and how it can exist in very definite factors, for all things are essentially energy. The proper understanding of conception in the mind will be of great value to you in the future, in the corrective therapies which are necessary, not only in your own life, but in the other lives which you may contact in your earth plane existence. The knowledge and wisdom which is incurred by the proper understanding of the laws of vibration, of harmonic and frequency expression, will give you, shall I say, a power or a dominion which has heretofore been confined only in the more highly evolved minds of such men as Jesus, Buddha and other spiritual leaders and healers.

In the realm of healing itself, there is considerable confliction and mysticism, which should definitely be cleared. The very existence of wisdom of the more highly evolved nature in a man's mind, immediately links him with the Superconsciousness; and in this process he therefore begins to bring into expression in his world the whole dimensional creation, which is compounded of fractions of Divine Intellect, which will immediately rectify the condition of all things about him. This improvement will also be reflected in more personal contacts with the individual. In the elements of your every day life, it is not necessary to indulge in hocus-pocus or manipulations and contortions of the body; nor is it necessary to symbolize such expressions in the votive sequences, called spiritual philosophies, as they exist in the church. Such things are only autosuggestive in their nature for they bring into the individual's consciousness a train of thought or reaction, which will link him with a somewhat higher dimensional order of relationship.

In a later section of the Shamballas we shall devote some time to the exploration of a section which relates to these devotional expressions of mankind. With a better understanding of the proper function of symbolism, man will evolve from that fearful so-called esoterical or mystical state of consciousness, in which he indulges himself on the earth plane. The practices of symbolism in the churches, and as expressed in the more primitive jungle regions in the form of witchcraft and the lower elements of exorcism, are, in themselves, only autosuggestions which, in the chain reactions, are supposed to link the individual with his higher self. As a person more truly understands his higher self, it is quite obvious that these external or physical or material applications and autosuggestive measures will become more or less superficial in their nature. They are perhaps necessary in the dimension in which man has not yet evolved into an intelligent relationship with himself, in which he can think constructively.

It is also quite obvious, if you study human nature about you, that man is very loathe to think, or even try to think constructively. Into the fabric of his own mentality and into the philosophy of his own life, he is constantly interweaving the threads and the strands of other people's lives and philosophies. He does not form a complete and constructive philosophy purely from the higher dimensions of his own true nature. Thus he is a creature of a reactionary stance, and in no wise a person who can be said to think constructively. His everyday act of consciousness in his world about him is only relating him to the past experiences of his own self and of his fellowman, with the conjunction of the different experiences of his earth life. If he were able to transport himself for any length of time into the dimensions where his Superconsciousness is in contact with the higher dimensions of intelligence, and with the propagation of such intelligence in these dimensions, he would be a superman or a God, just as was Jesus.

Man thus would likewise be able to walk upon water, walk through walls of stone, and do many other of these seemingly miraculous things. It can also be said that in instantaneous moments, healings do take place in the human body, when in moments of tense psychic stress, the individual, somehow or other for a very brief and fleeting instant, separates himself from the conscious objectivism of his own mind; and thus he lets the flood gates down to his own Superconscious Self. In such a moment, he may be healed or transported from some such physical condition. There is one more point which I should like to make, and that is the point of personal identity.

In these different transmissions which have been given to you, whether you yourself were in these planes and dimensions of Shamballa, or whether individuals were brought into your consciousness and so recorded in a dimension somewhat more closely related to your own earth plane, I will say that in all cases, any of us who have delivered these transmissions, would like to be thoroughly and completely separated from the identity of self, by the earth man. In no way did we try to impinge the inflections of what might be termed personal philosophies. It is obvious that in the great libraries where countless thousands of books are lying unread on the shelves, man is indeed portrayed in his own particular state of evolution. While much knowledge can be gained by the reading of the different ways of life about the earth, this knowledge in itself is propounded from individuals and contains the individualistic element of concept. These books are thus either partially or wholly rejected, because they are in themselves only fractionally true.

In the earth dimension, as has been said, a man

can gain only a very small portion of the infinite knowledge and intelligence which he will gain in his numerous evolutions into the higher dimensions. His own Superconscious Mind, or his own individual God Self, is the redeeming and the all-inclusive element in his makeup and in his nature, which will constantly relate him to these higher dimensions. This, my friends, is the true concept of Christ. It is in no way to be confused with some individual who has lived on the earth planet at one time, and then expressed this same Christ relationship from His higher self to His fellow man. These elements of misunderstanding, entering into man's consciousness, confuse him with his own true self. The Christ of Jesus, and as Jesus expressed this Christ on the earth in the miraculous happenings and dispensations of spiritual wisdom, can become the same translation of the infinite wisdom in your own life, if you would so evolve that you could conceive these principles into your own relationship.

In your own future evolutions and flights into these higher dimensions, you will learn to do so, just as Jesus did; then you may desire to go back into some terrestrial plane, such as the earth, to try to teach man in a similar way. It is also quite apparent, if you will study your history, that such men as Jesus have met with a great deal of very strong criticism; and this criticism sometimes assumed such proportions that it destroyed the physical expression of the individual, so that he was no longer able to continue his work on the earth plane. It is therefore quite obvious that man, who has induced these numerous guilt complexes or unadjusted thought patterns into his nature, may be unable to substantiate any portion of a higher degree of intelligence or concept in his own nature; and, like a beast of the night who is searching or stalking for his prey, so man, in searching for liberation from his physical desires in the terrestrial planes, becomes like the stalking beast of the night; and being fearful of the bright Light of Truth with which he is entirely unfamiliar, he may immediately become so fearful that he will wish to destroy it.

However, dear friends, I do not wish to enter into any more philosophies here which might tend to confuse you or lead you into fields of concept which you would be unable to assimilate at this particular time. Do think over these ideas about atomic structures and frequency relationship.

Try to see the different planes or dimensions of God's infinite expression, as they revolve and remanifest themselves down and down and down into the countless number of dimensions which arise in the somewhat natural sequence and order. You will see in each one of these dimensions vast worlds, or planetary systems, which might be called astral worlds or terrestrial planetary systems. But in the general summation and conclusion of your ideologies, for the moment at least, you have begun to gain a more basic concept and pattern of God's infinite wisdom, and the division of His infinite self into the more finite structures of the great cosmic and celestial universes. So until such time, dear ones, we await your pleasure for the further dispensation of spiritual knowledge into your earth plane.

CHAPTER 73

Greetings to the people of the earth and to you personally. Welcome back to Aureleus, and do not be too surprised at finding yourself standing in a section of this great city, which for a moment appears to you to be something like the section of the Egyptian architecture and civilization which you previously visited. Until your eyes become more accustomed to what is around you, I shall first identify myself as an individual who lived on the earth in the Grecian or Hellenic era, and served humanity as an historian, identified at that time by the name of Plutarch. Therefore, I have been most happy to accept the commission of conducting you on your next tour into this section of the great city. It has been purposely saved for one of the last portions of this transmission; and we wish to thank you one and all for being so patient with us while we gave the various transmissions from the different scientists and philosophers who have lived on your earth at different times. It is most necessary that you clearly evaluate and place within your minds the proper concepts of your relationship to these higher dimensions.

Now that you are becoming more accustomed to the brilliance and to the beauty about you, we shall go more into the actual investigation of these beautiful surroundings.

As you see, you are seated in a beautiful tropical garden, and before you appears to be a huge Egyptian temple. Although similar, there are some differences, however, which you will notice in the construction between these and the Egyptian temples. These great temples and buildings and pavements and all which you see about you are factual presentations of the buildings which are now, and have been in existence in your own Western Hemisphere. I am referring to the land which lies between the Mexican border of your United States and the southern dimensions of Peru and Ecuador, in South America, particularly in the area around Mexico City and in the Yucatan Peninsula. There you will find today the remnants of a vast and beautiful civilization, that is equaled only by the Egyptian or by some of the civilizations which existed in India.

In the science of archaeology, as it exists in the earth concepts of today, there has been much labor to uncover and to classify the civilizations of the different periods and epochs of time; yet there are still many gaps in these histories and much information that is yet missing. Consequently, it is apparent that in bridging these various eras and epochs of time in civilization, it indeed presents a varied and complex problem to properly integrate these different times and periods in your own concept. It is for these purposes, as you look about you and see the beautiful buildings, that I shall go somewhat into the background of this civilization, to see how it evolved into its height and glory, as it existed more than one thousand years or so before the time of the man Jesus. It was not built, as was commonly supposed, from the migrant population of Atlantis; instead, it actually was conceived and built as a direct interpretation of the artisans and craftsmen under the direction of an Egyptian, who was known to the Toltecs as Quetzacoatl, or The Many Feathered Serpent.

In order to learn more accurately how these civilizations existed on your earth during that era, we shall put aside, momentarily, the Aryan concept of the Shamballa, and go back to the period about 160,000 years ago. At that time the remnants of the Chinese race—remnants from Mars were struggling for survival on the plains of China. Out in the middle of the Pacific Ocean at the same time was another huge continent, which is known in your language of today as Lemuria. It was on this continent that a migrant colony from a planet by the same name landed and started a civilization, and so built a great city, bearing the same name, on the edge of this continent.

This huge civilization flourished for some 50,000 years or so, until the passing of a great star, as was described to you by Nurel, (in your 'Truth About Mars' book), causing this great continent of Lemuria, like many other portions of land, to sink beneath the waters, and others rising to take their place. However, before this destruction, the great civilization of Lemuria had succeeded in penetrating different portions of the planet, and in teaching the various peoples of those sections some fragments of civilization, in the realms and dimensions of architecture, science, religion, and various other kindred arts and sciences. One of these sections which had been penetrated by the Lemurian civilization is known today as Mexico and also the borderland of the Western Hemisphere of the United States, west of the Sierra Nevada Mountains.

Later, after the sinking of the continent of Lemuria, this civilization became rather decadent in nature and gradually, through thousands of years, began reverting into a rather primitive state of consciousness, without the supervision of the cultural natures of the instinctive forces from this Lemurian culture. This Mayan civilization, as it existed on the portion of the continent known as Mexico, was particularly outstanding in its exhibition of beautiful cities as well as great culture and refinement. However, it was not too outstanding or striking in its own dimensional growth.

Now we shall pause for a moment and inspect the other side of the American continent and go into what in now known as the Atlantic Ocean. There also existed another continent which is known to your day and time as Atlantis. It was another penetration of Lemuria, which set up a wonderful and beautiful civilization which survived the sinking of Lemuria, and did not sink beneath the waves until it was destroyed by the wrong use of atomic power, about 12,000 or 14,000 years before the coming of Jesus. It is important to remember this Atlantean period of civilization, in order to understand the beginning of Egyptian cultures.

As was pointed out in previous transmissions, the Aryan races had migrated into the various regions known as Chaldea, Assyria, Egypt, and Abyssinia. So it was that the artisans, the priests, and various other intellects from Atlantis, many thousands of years before its sinking beneath the waves, had penetrated into Egypt and there had found these migrants from the Aryan race living in various states of civilization. Thus it was that the cultures of the Atlanteans became thoroughly permeated and infused into the life of the Egyptian cultures during the many thousands of years of the dynasties of the pharaohs, after the time of Osiris, by the migrant priests from Atlantis. The Egyptian culture which sprang into existence is today one of the greatest and most mysterious semi-extinct civilizations on the face of your planet. We shall take, for example, the temple of Karnak, or Thebes, in the middle portion of Egypt. It is one of the great wonders of the world, with its diameter of about twenty-three miles and its one hundred great entrances or gateways.

The pyramids, whether the largest at Gizeh, built by Cheops, or any of several others, are all masterpieces of geometrical design, in which we can find examples of a perfectly squared circle, which exists in the exact meridian, or the parallax of magnetic flux which surrounds the earth. These temples and pyramids reflect to the utmost degree a much higher epitome of science, in both astrophysics and geophysics, than has yet been exhibited in your modern world.

There are other factors which we shall point out to you from time to time, which relate to this civilization of Egypt, for example, the similarity to the appearance of the temples in the Yucatan Peninsula and to many of the gods or the personages of deification, worshipped by these ancient people; and so it is quite natural that there must have been some connection, and this is quite true. We shall therefore begin approximately 3800 years ago, or 1800 before the advent of the Avatar Jesus, into the Holy Land of Galilee.

There was a great Egyptian architect known by the name of Amenhotep, who helped to construct the Egyptian temple of Karnak or Thebes, who propounded into the lives of the Egyptians of that time a great deal of the wonder and fabulous science which you see still existing in your day. This man was a mystic, a great man in many ways, who heard the call from the higher dimensions about the need of the decadent civilization of the Mayans. He therefore gathered about himself a great band of artisans of different natures and of different types; and as you study your Egyptian histories, you know that the Egyptians were very clever in the artifacts of stone. They had saws having teeth made of precious stones, and their science of copper and bronze was of such nature that they could construct tools which were even harder than your steel tools of today. Their science extended into the dimensions of vibronics and sound therapy, of which you know little, a knowledge which was very valuable to the Egyptians at that time.

In constructing these great temples and pyramids, they needed a great deal of stone, often limestone, but most preferably sandstone. Sandstone, when it is first cut from the mother earth, is of a rather soft nature; however, it hardens through the passage of time. The Egyptians knew that by going to the face of a large limestone or sandstone cliff, they could drive a series of long metal rods into it. Then, gathering together a large number of people, they would sing a certain chant, or they would harmonize on a single tone, which would vibrate the rods so that a large portion of the cliff would be broken off.

If you remember, Caruso would sit at a table, tap a glass by his side, find the note to which the glass vibrated, then sing this note loudly enough to cause the glass to fly into a thousand fragments. Exactly the same principle was used by the Egyptians to break off great portions of these cliffs, and to break these great portions into rude semblances of the square stones, which were later perfectly trued by the saws and other implements of their understanding.

Now Amenhotep gathered together a great band of these very advanced artisans and craftsmen of different cultures; and taking their families and their goats and their other animals with them, they began a long trip across the various countries between them and the coast of China. Their journey led them on up through what was ancient Assyria and Chaldea. As they went, they left behind them numerous minglings of their culture, in the races of people which they found along the way. This journey was necessarily slow and took a great number of years because of the many thousands of people involved and of the numerous animals and paraphernalia which was brought along with them, necessary to their life in this journey to the coast of China. They went through the upper portion of Mesopotamia, into Persia, and, skirting around the northern regions of Kashmir, they circumvented the northern portion of what is now known as Tibet. Going through the Mongolian plains, they finally arrived at the coast of China.

This brings into the proper place a story which is related to your own America. Your archaeologists and geologists have wondered why it is that great forests of redwoods are so abundant in a certain part of Oregon and California. They are found in only one other place in the world—the coast of China—and curiously enough, these trees started about 3800 years ago. Now I shall point out to you how these portions of trees arrived in your America.

On arriving at the coast of China, Amenhotep and his great band of followers found a forest of these sequoias, whose wood was the most valuable to be had at that time. They began to cut down these great trees with which to build vessels and rafts, which would transport them across the great sea, which was now empty of the continent of Lemuria, and had been for many thousands of years. There is a great current which swings across this vast ocean space, called the Japan Current, known to Amenhotep and his band. So after fabricating a great number of vessels from these great redwood logs, they ferried themselves across this vast ocean and landed along the coast, in the area now known as Humbolt County, near San Francisco. They dragged their vessels ashore, which became buried in the forests.

Now, you know that apparently dead and lifeless pieces of redwood are likely to grow if they have a piece of bark on them. It is quite likely that several pieces of wood from these vessels grew into trees. It may also be that the children, as well as the adults, had numerous pine cones or seeds of these trees, which scattered along the way; or perhaps the staves or other implements carved from these great trees were properly planted and flourished along the line of march, which followed along the coastal line from the area in which they had landed. So if you can trace on your map the area of these redwood trees, you will have the exact route which Amenhotep and his band of artisans traveled in their march to the land of Mexico.

Thus it is that about 3800 years ago, using an approximation of earth time, Amenhotep found himself in the general area of Mexico City, and later in the peninsula of Yucatan. There he succeeded in rebuilding the civilization and in teaching the decadent Mayan people the great and flourishing art of architecture, as it was known in Egypt.

That race of Egyptians, mingling as they did with the Mayans through the centuries that followed, became the race known as the Toltec people, who, of course, quite naturally brought with them many of the spiritual interpretations of the Egyptians. Thus it is that at the time of the invasion of Cortez and his Spaniards, these Toltecs, who had in their spiritual philosophies the Second Coming of Christ, believed Cortez, because of his fair skin, to be the Second Coming of this great God. These names, which are rather difficult to pronounce, may be found in your earth histories, if any of you are of a curious nature and wish further to explore to satisfy your curiosity.

Now the Toltecs are not to be confused with the Aztecs, who also exhibited the same type of civilization in the northern part of what is now Mexico. They too exhibited a very high degree of culture and civilization. However, at the time of the invasion of Cortez, a great deal of conflict had arisen between these two nations. There had been wars and strife, and already the jungle had been creeping about some of the cities of the Toltecs.

As you see these buildings and temples before you, here is one that is built on the face of a large pyramid, having three steps leading up to the main structure itself. As you look about, just as it exists in Yucatan today, you find not one, but three other temples which are built within it. The outside temple is about six stories high, with walls that are somewhat slanted. As you explore the various types of architecture, you will notice that the vast doorways are so placed that, as the sun streams in at the daytime, the stones in the interior of the building are so thoroughly warmed that they will radiate heat throughout the entire night.

There was also a provision made for the stormy times, whereby either wooden shutters could be thrown across these entrances and windows, or they were suitably covered with sheets of mica, mined from the hills, or cleverly matched panes of quartz. The art of window glass, as you know it in your time, was not expressed; but these people used the more natural mineral elements which were found in the hills and mountains about them. They exhibited something of the art of ceramics, in which they baked their various vessels in the fire, so that they became waterproof and indestructible. They also knew how to glaze and to make various types of porcelain. They were likewise very clever in the artifice of the manufacturing of silver and gold; and their clothing was very wonderfully interwoven and adorned with numerous gems, set in silver and gold.

The priest and the higher officials wore different types of bird plumage in the headdress and about their shoulders. The ruler of the whole nation, like the ruler of Egypt, was supposed to be of Divine conception; and he alone was permitted to wear a cape of feathers, which were taken from the bird of paradise.

Now you will begin to understand that obviously we can give you only a more or less superficial explanation of these great buildings. There is a twofold purpose for our brevity, inasmuch as we desire that the individual who reads these lines should be curiously inspired to pursue the various history books of the earth, which will more factually relate him to these great civilizations and eras of time. Much of this historical information is very factual in nature and has a high degree of relative truth. However, do bear in mind at all times that all sciences and philosophies, as they are expressed on your earth, as has been previously explained, are valuable only in their own time and in their own dimension, because all such sciences and philosophies have a certain element of human error in their composition; although unintentional, it is there nevertheless.

As far as they go, the histories of the world can be considered incomplete, and subject to additions and changes by future derivations into the science of archaeology. But generally speaking, as far as the philosophies and sciences are concerned, as they are entered into by mankind, one should be very careful to avoid a pitfall. The main point is that in no case should any of these sciences or philosophies be made some sort of a demigod in your personal expression of life. If you set up these ideas or philosophies in your own consciousness to the exclusion of anything else, you will become quite unbalanced; and you will be unable further to pursue a normal and integrated course in your evolution, until you have torn down such prefabricated notions of superiority as may have been expressed by some science, or by some philosopher who lived on the earth at some other time.

As we all so well know here in these centers—and as has been said in many cases—we are not too proud of what we left behind on your earth; and these things will become increasingly apparent to you in your evolution into the various dimensions. It is quite obvious, too, that the people of the earth must have some fragments of philosophy or science to cling to. They must express a certain degree of these elements into their everyday lives; otherwise they will lack the proper foundations and the elements of security; so these things are quite obviously very necessary.

You will bear in mind also that in all cases, as you have now begun to understand, the physical sciences on your earth are only partially factual. As has been explained to you, mass and energy are one and the same in their own respective and relative dimensions of expression to each other. The obvious constant interchange of energy between the opposite polarities is based on principles which were explained somewhat by Pericles and by other Grecians, as well as by some of the ancient Egyptians. There is much of this science contained in the Vedas or Brahmistic concepts of the early age, so that the derivation of truth, as it exists in different concepts, is by nature imperishable and will exist into eternity, and even beyond, for there is no eternity, since this word in itself is limiting. It is merely the way in which these truths are interwoven or distorted into unfactual and unrealistic elements in your daily lives, which made them obsessive or destructive in their general portent. And so until future transmissions, we bid you rest in peace.

CHAPTER 74

Greetings, dear ones; this is Brother Gamaliel. It is with a great deal of reluctance that I am bringing you one of the last and closing chapters from Hermes and the city of Aureleus. It has been with a good deal of pleasure that we have been able to be of some small service to you, as you have personally met and listened to the various interpreters of the earth science and philosophy, as they have existed in your more recent time. It is assumed that by now the interest of the reader will have reached a point where he will have searched the libraries and discovered to his own advantage and amazement that a great deal of wonderful history and truth can be gained by reading these books. It is also quite obvious that, numerous as our trips and discussions have been, we have presented to you only very small fragments and portions of these numerous lives and pages of historical events, as they were portrayed in the thousands of years of time in the sequence of evolution in the earth histories.

We began with the Egyptian and the Hindu, or the Brahmistic, concepts and philosophies, and concentrated more or less upon the philosophies and sciences as they were expressed and contained from the Grecian era, and on into your present time. There were many of these different philosophies; and in the semantics of their own interpretations, as was pointed out to you, these ideas, theosophies, theologies, and sciences were quite pertinent and relative to the dimension and time in which they were conceived. It was also pointed out that elements of truths of a spiritual nature were also sometimes contained and existed for posterity, and were valuable for men in a future day in evolution.

Let us review somewhat your previous visits, which were conducted by Plutarch, and the section which was devoted to the ancient civilization of the Mayans, the Toltecs, and the Aztecs, as they existed in your Western Hemisphere many thousands of years ago. You learned there that this civilization came into existence and was propagated by an Egyptian architect and philosopher of science, who migrated into this country at a period of time which antedated that of Jesus. This architect became later known as a god, called Quetzalcoatl, or the Feathered Serpent, because of his many talents and expressions of wisdom and intelligence in his dimensional world about him at that time.

There are, of course, quite obvious differences in the architecture of the so-called Mayan or Toltec civilization; yet as a general rule it can be assumed that, in their overall appearance, the types of pyramids or temples and various other buildings of these civilizations were quite similar in many ways to those of the Egyptian, as well as those of the Chaldean, Assyrian, and Babylonian. Just as in your day, the architects of your time portray quite obvious differences in their interpolations of architecture in the world about you; so it was in their time that they portrayed many differences; yet, as a whole, the architecture was strikingly of a design which can be termed a period.

Because of the limited time in which you are able to maintain continuity and appearance here in Aureleus and because of the vast size and magnitude of all that is about us here, we have been able to convey only a small fragment of the descriptions of these vast civilizations into the lines of your books, just as in the previous transmission that there was much which was not so thoroughly described.

Going a little further along into this discussion, we will say that at the advent of Cortez into Mexico, shortly after the time of Columbus, he found the beautiful city of Mexico actually floating upon the surface of a lake; and between the peninsula of Yucatan and Mexico City, in what appeared to be a jungle, was contained a world, or an empire, of fabulous historical treasures. There were hundreds of miles of roads which had been paved with what might be called flagstone, that is, with locking sections of stone. These roads wound about through the various mountain passes and through the jungle, but were either destroyed by the erosive nature of time, or were cracked and swallowed up and broken by the creeping jungle vines and trees that covered them.

Cortez also found great pyramids, existing at that time, which were equaled and excelled only by the pyramids of Egypt. These massive stone structures towered hundreds of feet into the air; and so, all in all, it can be said to have been a very wonderful and beautiful civilization. No doubt the people who had lived at that time were very highly advanced, with a vast amount of art and science at their command; so much so that the language written into the walls, and the stone buildings, which are still standing today, is almost imperishable, and is still a mystery to the archaeologists, who have been vainly trying to solve it for many years.

It could be noted too that the previous transmission did not deal with the more specific elements of the aboriginal cultures, as they existed in the tribes of

Indians, as they are erroneously called, through the northern reaches of your fair land of America. The Sioux Nation itself was an amalgamated federation of a number of nations, and was held thus by a somewhat democratic system of government. Likewise were the advanced races, the offshoots of the Mayans, called Seminoles. Going into the northern reaches of your country, around New York, we find the Iroquois, or the Five Civilized Nations, whose system of democracy had a tremendous influence in the construction of your United States. It was through William Penn and his treaties that a fuller understanding and a concept of this democracy was able to bring about a factual realization of the formation of the original Thirteen Colonies, for several signers of the Declaration of Independence were well acquainted with the Iroquois Nation.

This somewhat resembled the United Nations conclave of nations as it exists in New York today, which in itself presents somewhat of a strange parallel or paradox. The Iroquois Federation, consisting of five different nations, sent to the various councils, or the Long House, the delegates who were appointed by the nation; and these delegates presented the problems of the nation to the council. However, in the voting of such issues, the delegates were never permitted to vote upon the issue which concerned their own country. Thus it was that a very impartial and a very objective conclusion was reached in the solutions of these problems.

We might contrast that procedure to the numerous interjections of negations in the United Nations, by the great nation across the sea, which has rendered your United Nations conclave almost useless, by the constant refusal of acceptance of such modification of political sciences as they exist in your world today.

So in going into these various factions, we saw some of the works of a long line of Greek philosophers, the first of whom was Thales, who lived about 600 B.C., and who expounded the theory that the generation of all things sprang from the common substance, water. There were parallels, such as Seneca, who shortly after the time of Jesus, was forced to commit suicide just as was Socrates, due to a fancied plot against the Emperor Nero at that time. It was in the era before Jesus that we saw Aesop, as he wrote down his philosophies, which have existed as "Aesop's Fables" in a modern version of your time. There were others, such as Euclid, who gave mathematical postulations and theories, which are somewhat basic concepts even into your time. It was Hippocrates who first concluded many of the concepts which are still quite relevant into your time and day. It was he who first disproved that epilepsy was a religious visitation and, instead, proved that it was an organic disturbance.

Here again I might point out to you that many of these recent philosophies or truths brought into realization were only expressions which have been conceived in different eras in past ages, not only on your earth, but on other planets. For example, Dr. William Harvey was given credit for discovering the circulation of the blood; but that was known even at the time of Cleopatra and the Ramses dynasties, when the process of embalming used was quite similar to that of your own time, in which they drained the blood from the veins and arteries and replaced it with a homogenous substance, which ossified the surrounding tissues that then took on a parchment or a stone-like structure.

I might point out, too, that frequently a great deal

of false credit has been given to the so-called inventions of your time. Many of the basic concepts of truth in many branches of science and philosophy have been in no wise completely indigenous to your place or time; instead, they have been postulated and brought into a form of existence in many ages. They may not have contained exactly the same elements, or combined the actual elements of existence of that time; but the basic elements of such truths have remained with man; and it is obvious by now that you will have realized that the continuity of expression in these interpolations of knowledge and wisdom on your earth have been brought over to you, and with you, from other realms and dimensions, which we call spiritual or celestial.

As in the case of Isaac Newton, the theories of calculus and mathematics and the theory of corpuscular light, which he expounded, were later displaced and modified to a large extent by Planck and Einstein. Incidentally, I might say that the science of mathematics and calculus and the various geometrical and other forms of expression existing in your world today is in itself merely another channel whereby man reaches some form of a universal concept. The science of mathematics, as it exists now in many of its numerous branches, will progress to further heights or will disappear entirely from your concept, to be replaced by other concepts, which will be much more functional factors in your relationships to the future dimensions into which you are evolving and with which you are so vitally concerned.

I might say that to bear out the truth of this statement, we shall give an example; as Max Planck expounded the theory of transference of energy, not until his time was it universally accepted that energy was absorbed or admitted in somewhat of a regular fashion. However, Planck expounded the theory that such energy could be transmitted from one particular thing into another only according to a certain equation, which was called the Planck's constant, or the more commonly termed Derivation of Quantum.

I would like to say that in the time of Jesus, when He approached the leper, He did not say, "God, I know that $X + Y$ over E equals Pi," and that the leper must be healed by this formula. Nor did He say when He approached the blind man near the Well of Rebecca, as He put mud over his eyes, "25 x 8 over 29 E," and therefore this man's eyes were healed. This was to Planck simply a way in which he could conceive energy being transmitted from one dimension to another; consequently he must have these figures thus placed in his mind. In the future day you will see such sciences and philosophies factually replaced by others, which are much more relative to the dimension in which you find yourself.

In case that by now you are throwing up your hands in a somewhat fearful or horrified manner and saying that we are telling you that your philosophies and understandings are of no value, and you are wondering what you must do to replace them; to you I say, dear brothers, even if you tried to tear out these philosophies and understanding of the nature of the world about you at the time in which you live, if you should begin this very instant and continue for the rest of your life, you would be very unsuccessful. With a moment's thought you will see that you are in this world and of this world simply as a product of your own conception; and you will not evolve into another dimension until these concepts are further enlarged upon or have been replaced. These concepts which you have with you now relate to your own dimension and to your own time; and you have conceived them from numerous reincarnations in similar dimensions. They are as much a part of you as your arms and legs. Just as the crab and the lobster will grow a new claw if one is dislodged by an accident, so you too, in your evolutions, must displace all of these elements in your thinking by others.

The point I am trying to make is simply that you should not make demigods of the sciences or philosophies of the life about you. Likewise should you not misconstrue the elements of the material world in which you are living, as being the dominant and factual elements which will be in your life in future evolutions. Your life, as it exists today, was not the life of your grandmother or your grandfather. The average city or suburban dweller goes to the grocery store frequently; in fact, he literally lives from paper bags. Not so with your grandparents; they tilled the soil and milked the cows and took the vegetables directly from the soil itself.

You see thus that, in an overall pattern or a sequence of evolution, things are arrived at rather slowly. It would indeed be very harmful to you, to attempt to replace the philosophies and ideologies that you have conceived in your own dimension at the present time. However, it does not mean that you cannot begin to form elements of universal concepts and perceptions within yourselves. You can begin rightly to place all of these philosophies and elements, as they exist with you today, in their proper relation to you, in their factional orders of sequence of evolution. They should in no wise be misconstrued as the integrating elements which will be with you at your arrival in some future evolution, by which you can call yourself a spiritual being of some highly evolved nature. In that day and in that age, you will understand all of the elements in which you are now in a much broader and more universal fashion; and they will be interrelated and interwoven with other dimensional factors, so that you will instantly perceive, to a very high degree, a great deal of the tremendous cosmic and celestial universe around you.

Never attempt, however, in the postulation of concepts in your mind at this time, to think that you ever arrive at a concept in which you will instantly perceive all things at all times; only God can do that. It might be that in your return to God, you may be an integrational faction of conceiving a part of this universal concept. However, as this is beyond your realm of understanding at this time, do not attempt to go into these extreme abstract orders of concepts. They would only induce a neurotic pattern of frustration in your mind. Accept only the things which come to you from day to day, in the value and in the order in which they are received and as they are manifested. You might say that they are the blessings of God, and He is the actual, the ultimate, who is the originator and the conceiving force in all of the elements about you. It is down through the many dimensions in which we have arrived and concluded, that we are trying to explain to you that you will have, as we say, mailmen or delivery boys who will help you to arrive at some more of the concepts in your own personal philosophies.

Yes, you may pray to God, and you may believe that you are actually receiving a message from God, or that you may actually be seeing Christ. This is in itself a difference of opinion. As has been pointed out, God is completely universal and the originator of all things, and He lives in countless and numerous dimensions. It is quite obvious by now that He is not a personal God, nor is He contained in a personal being, as you might visualize in your mind. This

675

obvious concept must necessarily conclude you to believe that we must all participate in the general and unified theology of the cosmic universes. The acceptance of man into these different dimensions is such that he does so with his own will and volition, and with the understanding and with the elements of preconception which will enable him to make the various transitions or evolutions or reincarnations into these dimensions.

For the future, shape the destiny of your thinking into whatever channels that you may feel intuitively inclined to pursue. Always be conscious and cognizant of the great spiritual force within you, which is sometimes called the Still Small Voice. In the pursuance of your daily life, accept the various orders of experience as they come to you in a proper related concept, knowing that they are necessarily only elements of the experimental nature of life, as it exists with you in this terrestrial dimension. If your concept contains the elements of future evolution into higher dimensions, the possibility that you can become something more than what you really are, a creature sometimes called a victim of circumstance, do not let the false doctrines of this fatalistic concept enter into your mind. You must and you do, in all sequences of your experience, actually dominate to the utmost degree all of the proper integrational factors of dimensional precepts and concepts into your nature; and with the inception of these concepts, it is quite likely that you will incarnate into these dimensions.

The acceptance of life, as it is portrayed by the average individual upon the streets and highways and byways of your earth, is quite unrealistic, primitive, and elemental. You may find people who express the idea, "I live only once and I am going to get the most out of it while I am here." This is very idiotic and unrealistic in its portent and nature; and even those who say these things do not actually believe in them. If they did, they would very quickly change. However, I see that I have, in a sense of the word, repeated a great deal of what has previously been given. I would not have it thought for one moment that this book was becoming monotonous, or that we had reached a stalemate.

For the purpose of stimulating and increasing the interest of the individual, we shall therefore close this section of our discussions and explorations into the celestial and astral Shamballas, so that we can more factually acquaint you with these different laws and orders of the higher laws of spiritual interpretations. I would have you know, however, that we have striven to the utmost of our capacity to render to you in the parlance of your own dimension and in the nomenclature which is most understandable, not only to the layman but to the scientist, the existence of what is called space and the universal cosmos.

It is quite obvious, however, that this is a very infinitesimal part of what is actually in existence. We regret that at this time we do not have the proper terrestrial mechanism to bring these things to you on the movie screen. Do not think for one moment that there are not forces in existence that could bring into your world at this time a tremendous amount of what has been called physical phenomena or of such phenomenal nature that observers would see the celestial manifestations happening before their eyes. We here in the higher portals know of such supernormal phenomena of a psychic nature which is beyond the realm and dimension of any individual's understanding.

The end result, however, would be very damaging,

and it is not intelligent to bring to a person that which is beyond his concept of understanding, when at time of stress or emphasis the individual must accept any concept of truth as it is portrayed to him. We can, if he so desires, bring it into his mind and consciousness; but in the ultimate end, it is he who is ready to accept these things; and in accepting, to make such an attempt in an analytical equation in the process of his mind, whereby he can actually integrate them into his personal philosophy of life. Thus it is that he himself brings about a more unified condition of acceptance.

Frequently people get on their knees and pray, believing that they are praying to some supernormal or supernatural being, whom they call God. They must realize, factually, that they are not praying to some supernatural being of such a nature. As you know now, God manifests Himself in all directions and in all dimensions. Therefore the individual must pray only to the Divine Consciousness which is within him. As Jesus said, "The Father and I are one and the same," a statement He meant for all mankind when He stressed the Kingdom of Heaven within. Therefore if God is within, why does man pray to some far-off supernatural being?

You must realize also that even the most brief moments of intercession in which you contact your Divine Consciousness are of tremendous benefit to you in your material world; and as a natural consequence in such contacts with your Superconscious Self you will immediately see the effects of this contact in your daily life. Thus it is you will say that God has answered your prayers; but in reality you have manifested only a portion of your own Superconsciousness into your daily life. In the knowledge and wisdom which is within you, you can contain in your

Superconscious Mind all of the elements which are of the most Divine Nature of God Himself.

The creative qualities and the regenerative processes of the body are also transferred in another dimensional relationship into your body. Thus your body rebuilds and regenerates itself without your conscious volition or will; consequently, even the most brief and the most casual contacts with your Superconscious Self will, in all cases, be your Intercessor. It also means that even such brief moments of personal contact with the Superconsciousness will bring you into a direct alignment and into more factual continuity with the more evolutionary processes in the reconstruction of your own objective consciousness, as well as in the replacement of some of the spurious or negative wave forms or vortexes within your psychic body.

As a result, by the end of some earth lifetime, in which you have made possible a few such contacts with your Superconscious Self and have seen the results in your daily life, you will indeed begin to believe that there is such a thing as you call God. You have not yet developed to a point where you believe and can see this God existing in yourself; however, it is this actual God Self which is in contact with the Universal Consciousness, not only of the supreme God, but also in contact with the God likeness of all fellow men, as they exist in all terrestrial as well as in all spiritual dimensions which are above you.

The same processes in reverse are used in contacting the lower elements. The wave structures of your psychic body link you also into the lower astral dimensions of consciousness, and thus relate you with the direct consequence of these negative expressions. All of this I believe has been explained to you in different words and by different persons; yet, in the end, these principles are inviolate and are absolute in their nature. They cannot be changed, for to change them would be like trying to change God Himself, who created these things in the evolutionary nature of man; and since God is contained in the concepts of these things, so He must always be. In one previous transmission from the planet Venus, you were told that God has no laws, and this is indeed so, for God Himself is Law; and therefore He need pass no other laws, because God Himself contains all of the things which you might define as law, and which yet are only more basically the relationship of cause and effect.

This again is the equation of the polarities; and you, in your terrestrial dimension, are expressing the very extreme concept of this polarity. Consequently, since you exist in the elements of materialism, you have thus become the polarity farthest away from the supreme emanating source of God. Therefore the next and most direct approach, as it has been explained to you, will always be through the personal Comforter who will always be your Intercessor. This concept has been warped and distorted to include only one person, rather than you yourself. The damage of this concept has, as a consequence, a great and far-reaching nature; and one which you must spend many evolutions to outgrow, unless you take very constructive thought and action in your present daily life to eliminate that false concept from your philosophy of life.

The very process of evolution and life itself requires that you gain all of the infinite aspects of God's nature by relating yourself into the actual experience of dimensional contacts. It is quite obvious that if you have a broken leg, you yourself must have the leg set and you must wait the proper time for it to heal before walking upon it. This is cause and effect. In like manner, if you incur negative indispositions, you must also bring in the relationships which are of the most proper corrective nature, to supplant the negative influences which have been impounded within you.

We here in Aureleus, as in the other six centers, are most anxious to impress upon all of you these most vital and fundamental concepts in your relationships with your true innermost nature, so that you will always remember, in whatever circumstances and whatever condition or duress in which you may find yourself, you will immediately call upon the higher Superconsciousness of yourself. You will see your relationship truly placed in the divine concept of God's Mind, and you will become a factual, a working, and an integrated part of God, as He exists in the innumerable individuals called mankind. Until such time, dear ones, may you go about your way and your walk of life, with all of our love and our continued projection of the constructive energies of thought and mind and consciousness, into the dominion of the expression of your everyday life.

— Your Brother, Gamaliel.

CHAPTER 75

Greetings, dear ones. We here in the centers of Shamballa have heard certain questions arising from time to time in your minds as you have tried to evaluate and to place these truths within your minds. Now let me say that this is a healthy sign and a symptom that you are progressing. You can never properly evaluate truths, as they come to you through the doorway of experience, until they are properly placed within your mind, by integrating them with the necessary order of sequence, which is evolving about you in the dimension at your particular time. The problem of man's evolution in the numerous dimensions is in itself a very profound and, I need not say, a very advanced subject.

The truths which are being given you at this time are thousands of years in advance of the time in which other people of your time shall come into somewhat of a proper relationship to these truths. Therefore, do not fear a confounded feeling because you do not place within your minds a proper perspective of the objective values of these truths at this time. The philosophies of the earth today, just as they were in the time of Darwin and Mendel, are in themselves being constantly and repeatedly stressed, for the concepts were resolving in these individuals at their time in an effort to solve something of the riddle of man's nature. All philosophies and ideologies, whether they are scientific or spiritual interpolations on your earth

683

today, contain only small fractional elements of the truths which are relative to mankind at his particular state of evolution, and they are themselves even only partially factual.

The progress of the individual, whether in his physical reincarnation or in his spiritual evolution, is manifested in the contents or in the construction of the psychic body. You will see that this has a natural order of sequence or evolution, just as has everything about you. Your own physical body, in one lifetime, will be reincarnated or rebuilt perhaps as many as eight or ten times. Thus as you can see that the body has replaced the atomic constituents, for they are elemental forms of energy of the earth; and every atom is thus replaced within the physical body as a natural course of its evolution every so many years. This process is very gradual and you are not at any time aware of what is going on.

If you cut your finger, you will see that the healing process beings immediately. You have nothing to do with the sealing over or the coagulating of the blood and the gradual replacement of the damaged cells. Your finger will, in a few weeks time, present an entirely normal picture; and you will be unable to detect which one had been cut. The individual problem of man himself, as was pointed out, is somewhat different in his relationship to the infinite nature of God— if we can refer back to that much repeated concept, the infinite nature of God—for God expresses Himself finitely into numerous and countless dimensions. These in themselves are subjects which should be given a great deal of thought and research.

In the dimension of the animal and vegetable kingdom, as it exists in your world and in your dimension, here again God is expressing Himself just as He does in lower terrestrial or astral dimensions or worlds, in such forms and continuities as the regenerating of the species. This was only partially conceived by Darwin. He did not, in his consciousness on the earth, interweave the necessary spiritual concepts, which made it more easily understood that the plant and the animal life was not only concerned with its evolution on the earth at that time, but because it was essentially (and in essence) spirit, it too must incarnate in a natural order and sequence. The amoeba and the other small animals, such as your mice, are not concerned with the idea of self. They have a spiritual connection or linkage to another dimension, which you have called instinct. It is this intelligence or instinct which causes them to react and to forage about for food and in other ways seem to indicate a certain amount of an intelligence quotient.

We can say that the amoeba appears and reappears in the countless divisions of its body, as it generates on the earth, and has done so for many thousands and thousands of years. This minute microscopic bit of protoplasm does not have any personal identity; it is merely expressing God in another dimension and in other forms. It is at all times supported by the continuity of the spiritual dimensions above it. It may, being constructed of God's spiritual essence, revert into something of a great spiritual reservoir of divine energy or concept, and thus be reconstituted in another dimensional form in some other dimension. This in itself is part of the process of evolution of the species, as they are thus constantly being returned into the spiritual dimensions, as well as into the terrestrial dimensions with which you are somewhat associated.

The main dividing line between man and the species of plant and animal life, as they exist in your dimension, exists also in the concept of God's own divine intelligent nature; and God Himself is expressed in man alone, the original divine concept of God being personalized or individualized in each and every individual. These individuals are countless and without number; so here again God becomes infinite.

Reverting to the original concept of the Life Cycle, it was brought into existence as a divine concept, or the great All-Pervading Intelligence of God. You might picture this All-Pervading Intelligence as something of a ring, or a halo of very beautiful spiritual Light, which transcends any appearances of Light which you know in the transmissional or directional forces of energy on your earth. This Light is of such intense nature that you would be totally unable to perceive it in the normal structures of your physical body. Just as we here in these centers would appear to you as flaming individuals or supernatural beings, so we too very often see those who are more advanced than we, appear to us as flaming individuals, who are somewhat without the form of the human body, as you would have associated us.

Now it is quite easy to see that since this energy is of tremendously advanced spiritual form, it could not exist in a lower dimension. It may contain all of the ideas and the elements of its future lives, since it was compounded of God's own infinite nature, which knows of all the things of which it was universally compounded. Just as you may see a picture or have a description of some city, such as Venice, Italy, yet the appearance seen in your physical form with your physical eye would give you a different picture of the city. So it is with the sequence of your evolutions; you are thus within yourself becoming so individualized in your nature that you may thoroughly understand all the infinite greatness of God's Mind.

Now the Life Cycle, as you have pictured it in your

mind, is a circle of very beautiful brilliant intense Light. If you could see into it clairvoyantly, it would contain within itself the vastness and the infinity of your reincarnations and evolutions. These things in themselves would not necessarily be the actualities of happenings as they are expressed in your earth life. However, although there may be a postman or a brick-layer or a carpenter in your dimensional form of expression, he need not necessarily reincarnate back into the earth and become a postman or a carpenter. This conclusion is quite illogical. It merely means that each of these tradesmen, whether doctor or nurse, professor or teacher, is only learning his proper relationship to the dimension in which he is thus expressing himself. The difference here is expressed into the psychic body, wherein, with each succeeding evoltuion and generation, the psychic body, like the physical body, is constantly being replaced and rebuilt.

In your final and concluding initiations into the higher spheres, which are somewhat comparable to Shamballa, you will have gone through such energy transformation which will completely eliminate the last vestiges of this old psychic body, because it is primarily, in the beginning, constructed of the elements which began with your first function as a human being in some terrestrial dimension. In the beginning, man, as he first started in perhaps the lowest order, would quite naturally express himself in the exact opposite to that of entering into this ring of celestial experiences, which you have called the Life Cycle.

We say that the consciousness of God, as it is contained in the spiritual circle or cycle of man's own individuality, can be likened somewhat to his umbilical cord. He maintains this constant inflow of Divine Energy into his own spiritual Life Cycle at all times.

This he must do. The various dimensional and factional orders of integration in God's infinite universe are so contained that each one is supported from outside the other by succeeding higher realms of consciousness. Now you will begin to understand why we say that it is not the act of committing some good or some sin that is of importance. The utmost importance is contained in the reaction which takes place within your mind, which is reflected and thus becomes a constructive element or a defective wave form or impingement, within your psychic body. If this is of evil consequence, with the repetition of the reflections and impingements of these evil consequences into your psychic body, you will become the creature which is thus formed and reformed, as far as the proper sequence of your evolutions are concerned; and thus you will relegate yourself into the lower astral orders.

If these acts of consciousness, which are contained in the daily life in the world in which you find yourself, can be said to be of a constructive nature, or are even only superficially related to your dimension, these too will be impinged and become a part of your psychic body. Therefore, when you find yourself in the spiritual dimensions and are devoid of the flesh, your psychic body will be you. Here again you must always remember that the psychic self, like the spiritual self, is connected with God through a spiritual umbilical cord; so that you are always connected with your spiritual consciousness by an umbilical cord. This can be called frequency vibration or relationship. It means that at all times you are being supported in your own psychic body by the inflow of energy or wisdom, as it is expressed within the psychic cycle itself.

The various wave forms, as they are called—experiences in your psychic body—would cease to exist, if they were not thus supported in some way from the inflow of celestial energies from some other dimensions. You may wonder why a person of a vile and evil nature has not thus automatically destroyed himself, because now God's wisdom cannot flow into him through his own spiritual self. The principle which prevents this self-destruction is called the personal Redeemer or Savior. You have all heard it said that the doorway to reformation is never closed here or hereafter, and this statement is quite true.

It makes little difference to the All-Pervading God Force, which comes through the Superconsciousness of the individual that one progresses lower and lower into the astral dimensions in his psychic conscious. That fact is of small consequence in an overall sense to the All-Pervading God Force which created this individual. It simply means a matter of time. The psychic body, which contains the acts and consciousness of the individual himself within itself, if he continues his reversion into the astral orders or dimensions, will finally arrive at such a place that this psychic body must either revert into the complete absolute of the cosmic consciousness, or it must again begin an evolution or reinstatement of purpose of incarnations back into a more constructive sphere of consciousness.

This whole idea is one of great challenge to the absolute power of your conception. It may pose the question of just how vile or malformed and evil the psychic body of the individual can be, and yet, it can still reincarnate into some dimensional form, and re-enact the purpose and dominion of the evil crimes which is contained within the vileness of this consciousness. This is an absolute abstraction of the philosophy of idea of reincarnation. It simply means that nothing, *absolutely nothing,* is unsupported and unrealistic in the dimension in which it functions. Everything thus becomes, in the absolute or the abstract concept, a part of that All-Pervading, All-Permeating, and All-Intelligent God Force itself.

Everything is a part of the infinity of God's nature; and thus you may say that God may thus be evil and yet express the continuity and form of law and order into the dimensional structures that are always contained within the intelligence of the Life Cycle of the individual. In other words, a person who has so constructed in his psychic body the evil forces of his nature to such a point, that the life force will thus reach a conclusion that he will either call upon his spiritual nature and begin his climb back through reincarnations, or he will pass into the universal cosmos of energy transformation, or disintegration, if I can use this word rather loosely. God has a certain way, or a law and order, in which such things are properly regulated and made useful and intelligent. Thus all must return as an intelligent form, which can be reinstated into a dimensional form of expression with the divine and infinite nature of God Himself.

However, this whole principle is one of abstract nature. It should not be misconstrued by the individual on the earth so that he may say, after reading these lines, that because he contains much evil and vileness, he will continue on this path, thinking that if he goes far enough, he will thus be able to look upon his God and upon his inner self and in so doing be reinstated in the goodness of the more constructive purposes of his life. He will find, to his regret, that each act of vileness and destructiveness in his nature will be intensified tenfold in its strength, in the evolutions of his various reincarnations. In other words,

690

the individual must expend at least ten times as much constructive and useful purpose and intent into this world, as was originally expounded as a destructive evil intent or purpose. This is because the higher and innermost self lives in a dimension which is not quite so relative and intent in its nature, as is the physical self of the person in his lower state of evolution. Thus you can see that each evil act or thought or purpose must, in consequence, be fully rectified; it must be replaced and rebuilt by constructive wave forms, which will automatically relegate the individual into a higher relationship to the dimensions above him, as he progresses in his evolution.

You might see numerous examples of the fallaciousness of negative thinking about you on the earth plane today. You will see numerous people who have resolved their status of life, not only into physical deficiencies of disease and inadequacy, but also into their mental consciousness. They are completely devoid of any intelligent continuity. Their life is simply one of superficial laxity and indulgences into the superfluities of physical nature; and, in consequence, their bodies very often reflect these conditions of mind. They arrive at the middle or later portions of their lives with physical bodies atrophied or malformed into diseased conditions, which will cause them great pain and suffering.

There is another side which I would like to interject, which may be of some value to you in forming the more constructive precepts of evolution. This relates in a rather personal way, which I am pointing out with a two-fold purpose of solving one of the riddles of your own evolution. As the channel, you are at your present day, somewhat cognizant of what karma is, as it manifests itself into the body in different ways, to the psychic malformation of the psychic body. An individual may or may not be entirely responsible for the karmic conditions which are contained in the family relations of their own evolutions in dimensions at stated times. I am presenting this to you for the understanding that the individual, in reincarnating into the lower orders of his evolution, is not always sufficiently advanced, intellectually, to be able to determine or select the environment into which he reincarnates. He is motivated, primarily, with the idea that as long as he can get into life, he will do so. Thus he quite frequently makes the mistake of getting into the doorway of life in the material world which brings about him more of karma and suffering than he would be justly entitled to, had he used a little more care in his selection, and related himself a little more carefully in the dominion of frequency relationship and environmental factors which were reflected into this relationship.

This hasty error in itself will, in the course of his evolutions, be a great lesson to him; and it will thus manifest to him the right and the prerogative of reincarnation into the world into environmental factors of his environment, which will further the purpose of his life and his reincarnation in the service of mankind about him. In your biographies of the earth, you will notice that many musicians, statesmen, philosophers, artists and scientists came into the world, seemingly supported in their lives on the earth, and were made useful and constructive by the elements of parental influences; or their families had wealth, which enabled them to attend the necessary colleges and to obtain other advantages. There are other examples, too, which are, fortunately, not so numerous, in which the individual had to make a tremendous struggle against very adverse forces. These cases also must be taken individually to be more properly understood. But it must be remembered that they too are contained in the differences of the interpretations of life of the individual as he is so contained within the memory consciousness of the psychic body.

You have often wondered how it is that people, in a genealogical sequence, seem to manifest and remanifest themselves and thus relate themselves similar to branches upon a tree from the main stem. We say that there are, in your land of America today, a large number of people whom we shall call by the name of Smith. The name Smith itself has its origin in the antiquity of the more primitive civilizations, such as in the beginning of the history of England, and that the people themselves, manufactured the numerous weapons of war, as their armors and spears, as well as their various necessities of life; these were hand forged by numerous men who were called smithies. These tradesmen as you will see were occupied in the numerous trades and crafts; and in the different civilizations were countless and without number. They are, in your day and time, incarnated into your world in a natural genealogical order or sequence of evolution. They are attracted into the family of Smiths simply because they were smithies. This explains how through these different orders of sequence, as they are contained in the vibration and memory consciousness of the psychic body, the individual will reincarnate instinctively into the dimensions for which he seems to be best adapted and suited.

When Genghis Khan invaded Russia, Poland and Germany, he left behind him numerous children as well as deserters of his army. That is why you see the high cheek bones and the Mongolian aspects of the Russians as they exist today. They also build their buildings somewhat reminiscent of and portray the type of architecture to be seen in the Oriental coun-

693

tries.

We here in these Shamballas await your pleasure and disposition to reopen the next visitation into the remaining sections of expressions of Shamballa. You are asking our personal identity. Let us say that we are those whom you have received previously; we are the identities you might call Buddha, Maha Chohan, Maitreya, and others. Dear ones, until such future time,

— Shella.

Other works by Ernest L. Norman:

The Voice of Venus
The Voice of Eros
The Voice of Orion
The Voice of Muse

The Infinite Concept of Cosmic Creation
Cosmic Continuum
Infinite Perspectus
Infinite Contact
Truth About Mars
The Elysium (Parables)
The Anthenium   "
Magnetic Tape Lectures
Tempus Procedium
Tempus Invictus
Tempus Interludium Vols. I & II

Also a publication, now reprinted by
Unarius Publishing Company:
The True Life of Jesus of Nazareth (1899)

(The Sequel): The Story of the Little Red
Box